P9-DGV-535

# YOUR ATTITUDE IS SHOWING

## A PRIMER OF HUMAN RELATIONS

### Tenth Edition

## Sharon Lund O'Neil

University of Houston

## Elwood N. Chapman

JOB SKILLS
NETEFFECT SERIES

Prentice
Hall

Upper Saddle River, NJ 07458

Library of Congress Cataloging-in-Publication Data

O'Neil, Sharon Lund.
   Your attitude is showing : a primer of human relations.— 10th ed. / Sharon Lund O'Neil, Elwood N. Chapman.
      p.  cm.
   Authors' names appear in reverse order on 9th ed.
   Includes index.
   ISBN 0–13–022507–X
   1. Psychology, Industrial.   2. Industrial sociology.   3. Interpersonal relations.   I. Chapman, Elwood N.   II. Title.

HF5548.8 .C36   2001
158.7—dc21
                                                           2001036172

**Executive Editor:** Elizabeth Sugg
**Publisher:** Steve Helba
**Editorial Assistant:** Anita Rhodes
**Managing Editor:** Mary Carnis
**Production Editor:** Brian Hyland
**Director of Production and Manufacturing:** Bruce Johnson
**Manufacturing Buyer:** Cathleen Peterson
**Design Director:** Cheryl Asherman
**Cover Design:** Wanda España
**Cover Illustration/Photo:** David Ridley, SIS/Image.com (comedy/tragedy masks)
**Net Effect Series Design:** Rob Richman, La Fortezza Design Group
**Composition:** BookMasters, Inc.
**Full-Service Production Management:** BookMasters, Inc.
**Printer/Binder:** Phoenix Book Tech.

Pearson Education LTD.
Pearson Education Australia PTY, Limited
Pearson Education Singapore, Pte. Ltd
Pearson Education North Asia Ltd
Pearson Education Canada, Ltd.
Pearson Educación de Mexico, S.A. de C.V.
Pearson Education—Japan
Pearson Education Malaysia, Pte. Ltd
Pearson Education, Upper Saddle River, New Jersey

10  9  8  7  6  5  4  3  2  1
**ISBN 0-13-022507-X**

# Contents

# Preface

For over thirty years, the first nine editions of *Your Attitude Is Showing* have been used in the classroom and work place to train both new and experienced employees. Over one million copies of the book have been distributed. *Your Attitude Is Showing* remains one of the most highly regarded primers in the field of business human relations.

*Your Attitude Is Showing* has helped individuals of all ages and backgrounds play their human-relations roles with greater understanding and sensitivity. Everyone who seeks self-improvement will welcome this tenth edition.

In the tenth edition of *Your Attitude Is Showing*, readers will find new and updated materials in each of the chapters. A "Thought for the Day" has been added at the beginning of each chapter for the reader to ponder as the chapter is studied. At the end of each chapter is an "Attitude Box" that further reinforces one or more of the key concepts of the chapter. Readers are encouraged to refer to both the Thoughts for the Day and the Attitude Boxes on a regular basis. These short statements are provided to encourage the reader to stop and think about being more positive toward attitude improvement.

To further promote personal and professional development, readers of the book are encouraged to contemplate the end-of-chapter cases. Each case will give the reader a good opportunity to analyze a situation that represents an all-too-common reality in the workplace.

As you read and study *Your Attitude Is Showing*, keep in mind that people who balance their technical skills and knowledge base with human-relations competencies find greater on-the-job happiness, contribute more to the productivity of organizations, and, in general, have more successful careers and satisfying lives. And, remember, no matter what you do, *Your Attitude Is Showing!*

To the million plus readers who have made the first nine editions of *Your Attitude Is Showing* so popular, the authors, publisher, and editors extend our appreciation. We thank you and dedicate this tenth edition to you.

# About the Authors

Sharon Lund O'Neil, co-author of *Your Attitude Is Showing*, is a widely published author. Her human relations cases, based on the corporate work environment, are popular with both trainers and educators. With a common-sense approach to problem solving, she has led national professional and educational organizations and has been the recipient of many teaching awards. She holds a Ph.D. degree from the University of Illinois and is currently a professor at the University of Houston.

In Memoriam: Elwood N. Chapman, co-author of *Your Attitude Is Showing* and author of several other books, was known as "Mr. Attitude." He was praised for his friendly writing style and practical advice. People who knew "Chap" speak fondly of his concern for people. A former professor at Chaffey College, Chap was a nationally-known consultant and speaker.

# Introduction

This book could be appropriately subtitled *Gaining Personal Success in Business*, for nothing has more impact on career success than one's attitude. Illustrations like the one below will help you become more aware of the strong impact your attitude has on every aspect of your life. Each drawing shows an amoeba—a microscopic one-celled creature who is constantly changing in size and shape and who is often referred to as the lowest form of animal life. We hope the little amoeba will act as a reminder that, no matter where you are or what you are doing, *Your Attitude Is Showing.*

**"After all, I'm just an amoeba."**

# PART I

# Understanding Yourself

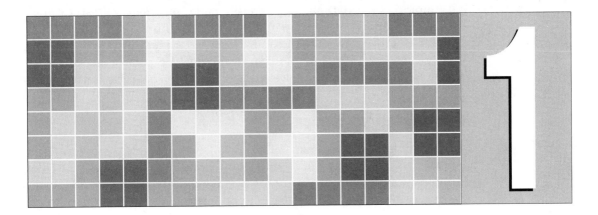

# You Can't Escape Human Relations

**"I've heard all that old stuff before."**

Thought for the Day: Relationships are only as good as your commitment to what you want them to be.

Most employees, even those with considerable experience, greatly under-estimate the importance of human relations in building their careers. They pass it off as nothing more than common sense—something one handles in-tuitively. They are blind to the significance of the subject because they wrongly assume they are automatically good at it. So what is *human relations?*

## Human Relations Basics

On the simplest level, human relations is being sociable, courteous, and adaptable. It is avoiding trouble with fellow workers. It is following the rules of simple etiquette. But as important as these qualities are to personal success, they only scratch the surface. Human relations is much more than be-having courteously so that people will like you. There is a second, more complex level.

Human relations is also knowing how to handle difficult problems when they arise. It is learning to work well under demanding and some-times unfair superiors. It is managing conflict effectively. It is understand-ing yourself and how you communicate with others. It is building and maintaining long-term relationships with family, friends, and co-workers. It is knowing how to restore a working relationship that has deteriorated. It is learning to live with your frustrations without hurting others or jeopardiz-ing your own career. It is communicating the right kind of attitude during an employment interview. It is the foundation upon which good manage-ment careers are built. In short, human relations is *building and maintain-ing* relationships in many directions, with many kinds of people, in both good and bad working environments.

## Positive Attitudes Appreciated

The most popular and productive people in any work environment are usu-ally those with the best attitudes. Their positive attitudes

- inject humor into what otherwise would be just work. Everyone misses these individuals when they are on vacation.

- add to the team spirit by "bonding" everyone together in a more posi-tive and productive mood. Many are unofficial leaders greatly appreci-ated by supervisors.

- make it easier for co-workers to maintain their upbeat attitudes. A posi-tive attitude, in turn, helps co-workers maintain productivity and en-hance their own careers.

Employees who are consistently negative put an added strain on their co-workers. Their negative attitudes

- make it more difficult for others (especially the supervisor) to stay positive. Because negative attitudes thwart creativity, everyone operates under a needless handicap.

- act like a spoiled apple in a barrel, causing fellow employees to lose their enthusiasm and motivation to contribute. (Why produce more when Jack or Judy gets by with being so negative?)

- repress the fun and harmless horseplay that would normally surface and make everyone feel better about what they are doing. It often takes many highly positive attitudes to offset one that is negative.

## Attitudes Travel

When others are making a big effort to remain positive in their work environment, a single negative attitude can act as a cloud over the entire atmosphere. Productivity can drop. Customers can be treated poorly. Positive employees may seek opportunities elsewhere. While not everyone can be an attitude "star," negative attitudes damage human relationships in the workplace. Those who find it difficult to remain positive are invited to concentrate on Chapters 3, 19, and 20.

## Productivity Outcomes

In the business world, human relations (attitude) is viewed best in terms of productivity because productivity is the goal of all group activity. Human relations, of course, is not a substitute for work; it cannot replace or camouflage poor performance. Employees are valued primarily for the amount and quality of work they turn out. Your employer will expect you to do your share of the work. And if you are interested in moving ahead, you will want to do more than your share. An employer will not be interested for long in an employee who has a great attitude but produces very little.

## Sensitivity Factors

But getting the work out is only one side of the coin. You should accomplish your work and still be sensitive to the needs of those who work with you. You should perform your work without trying to show up your fellow workers or antagonize them. You should carry your full load in such a way that others will be encouraged to follow rather than reject you.

No matter how ambitious or capable you are, you cannot become the kind of employee you want to be (or the kind of employee management wants you to be) without learning how to work effectively with people. It would be career suicide to join an organization and ignore the people who work around you. You simply cannot escape human relations.

Does this mean that you should deliberately set out to play a game of human relations on your new job? The answer depends upon what you mean by "playing a game."

If you mean that you should play up to those who can do you the most good and pay little attention to others, the answer is, of course, "no."

If you mean that you should devise a master strategy that will give you the breaks at the expense of other people, the answer is again "no."

If, however, you mean that you should sincerely do everything you can to build strong, friendly, and honest working relationships with all the people you work with—including those from diverse cultures—the answer is an unqualified "yes."

If this comes as a shock, think about it. Working hard is not enough in our modern society. It may have been thirty years ago, but it isn't today.

## Human Relations Responsibility

You, as a new or experienced employee, have a definite human-relations role to play. You can't ignore it. You can't postpone it.

From the moment you join an organization, you assume two responsibilities: (1) to do a job—the *best* job you can do with the work assigned to you—and (2) to get along with *all* the people to the best of your ability. It is the right combination of these two factors that spells success.

Perhaps you are a highly qualified, experienced employee happy in your present work environment. Or perhaps, after working a number of years for a particular company, you are making a career change. Or your firm eliminated your position and you are seeking a similar one elsewhere. Or you may be graduating from an educational institution soon, and you are preparing to launch your career. The possibilities are endless, but no matter what your personal condition is now or what it may be in the future, human relations will play a dominant role.

It would be wrong, of course, to say that the skills or abilities you possess are unimportant. If you are employed as an office manager, your computer competencies are vital. If you are employed as an apprentice machinist, your mechanical ability is important. If you are a registered nurse hoping to get into management, your professional training and background are vital. These skills helped you get where you are, and they will help you make progress.

But they are not enough. In order to make your education and experience work for you as effectively as possible, you must become competent in human relations. You must learn the technique of working with others.

Why? Because your behavior has a direct bearing on the efficiency of others. Because your contribution will not always be an individual contribution; it will often be a component of a team effort, and you will only be a part of the group. Because what you accomplish will be in direct proportion to how well you get along with the people who work with you, above you, or for you.

Almost everything you do will have an effect on other people. If the effect is good, people may do a better job. If the effect is bad, they will be less productive. Your personal work effort will not be enough. You should conduct yourself in such a manner that those who work with you and near you will also become effective. As you move into supervisory roles, you will be judged less on your personal productivity and more on the team you manage.

## Team Management

*Productivity* has become a significant word in business, industry, and government. Every organization operates either to make a profit or to reach a certain level of excellence.

Management has its own ways of measuring work quality and productivity. Some jobs are more easily measured than others. If you are employed as a factory worker, for example, your productivity is measured by the amount of work you perform over a certain time.

Some organizations employ time-study experts to measure the time required to perform a given task and to establish standards of performance. As an employee of such a company, you are expected to exceed this standard. If you are employed in a sales organization, for instance, you might be given a sales quota that you would be expected to reach or exceed.

The point is that everyone's productivity is measured. We must all live up to the standards that prevail in our particular business. There is some form of measurement or evaluation for every job.

## Work Contribution

Our value is measured not only by the actual work we do, but also by the contribution we make to the department as a whole. This is human relations as management sees it. Productivity is not only an individual matter, it is also a divisional or department matter. Management has discovered that the way people get along together has a great deal to do with departmental productivity.

Let us take the example of a checker in a supermarket. The productivity of a checker is usually measured in three ways: speed, accuracy, and relations with customers. But it doesn't stop there. Why? Because the way others react to this person has an influence on their own productivity, as well as on the productivity of the checker. If she (or he) is an excellent checker and measures above others in all three categories, one would think this person would be the best checker of all. But this is not necessarily true.

Let us assume that it is a peak period in the supermarket and all checkers are extremely busy. Shoppers are lined up in front of each check stand. One of the other checkers suddenly runs out of paper sacks and calls for our "superior" checker to toss him a few. What if our superior checker says, "Come and get 'em if you want 'em." What would happen? A psychological barrier would immediately arise between the two checkers. The checker requesting the bags would be embarrassed in front of the customers. And as a result, his speed, accuracy, and relations with customers would deteriorate. So even though our superior checker is exceptional in all three categories, she has hurt the total productivity of the operation. Nobody can beat her as far as doing her assigned job is concerned. However, she has failed to live up to good human-relations standards.

In other words, productivity is not only what you do yourself, it is also the influence—good or bad—you have on others. You not only have a job to perform, you have a contribution to make to your fellow employees. It is not a contribution that always comes easily. On occasion you may find it necessary to work effectively with someone you do not like. If you succeed, you have made a worthwhile contribution. If you fail, try to learn something from the experience and wait for another chance, for it is a challenge you should eventually meet successfully. The worker who keeps his (or her) personal productivity high, and at the same time is sensitive enough to have a beneficial influence on others, is the worker management will probably reward.

## The Power of Human Relations

Human relations knows no age or experience level. You may be a recent high school or college graduate starting your first job, a middle-aged person entering the labor market for the first time, a senior citizen taking up a new career, a housewife returning to a job left years ago, or a long-time career employee just promoted to a management position. Whatever your situation is, human relations will play a vital role in the years that lie ahead.

Once you understand that there is no escape from human relations, you will be in a position to capitalize on it and to receive the greatest compliment of all: to be recognized, perhaps by a supervisor or a fellow employee, as having the ability to work harmoniously with others. Your knowledge about human relations will have earned you that distinction.

> *What you accomplish can be magnified by the relationships you build in getting it accomplished.*

# Case 1

**"It's *who* you know that counts."**

# Reality

When Rod and two equally qualified people were hired at a fast-paced, in-
novative, high-tech firm, they knew there would be good promotion opportunities. Rod was pleased to be assigned to a department that was known
for its high productivity and teamwork. Rod's team leader told him how fortunate he was to get the assignment, and she quietly suggested that Rod
make a special effort to get along with everyone.

Rod worked hard and efficiently in his new job. However, he made several human-relations errors. For example, he was rather rude to a co-worker
who returned some borrowed files in three batches rather than all together.
Another time he complained that he had to take a late lunch because a fellow employee had failed to return on time. On still another occasion, he
openly expressed his displeasure when his workload was temporarily increased because a co-worker had to go home sick.

Only a few weeks had passed when the team leader called Rod into her
office for a serious talk. The team leader focused her remarks on the importance of getting along with co-workers instead of unintentionally rub-
bing them the wrong way. At the end of the discussion, Rod asked if his
work was satisfactory. The team leader told him that it was substantially
above average, but was quick to add that Rod's human-relations skills were
below par and needed improvement.

Some months later Rod heard that promotions had been given to the two
people who were hired at the same time as he was hired. He passed it off by
saying, "In this outfit, it isn't what you know but who you know that counts."

Was Rod justified in feeling this way? What might Rod's team leader
have done to help Rod with his human-relations problems? (For a suggested
answer, see page 224.)

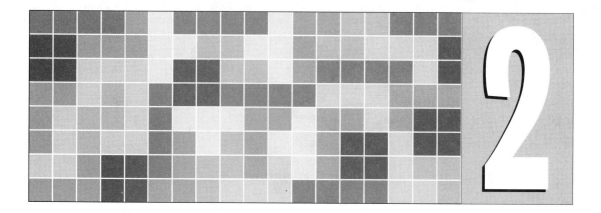

# Human Relations Can Make or Break You

"Me? A split personality?"

Thought for the Day: To question how you are being perceived is a healthy way to assess the effectiveness of your human relations skills.

As with most people, Chapter 1 may have raised several questions in your mind. In this chapter you will find answers to some of the most frequently asked questions that have human relations implications.

## How Significant Is Attitude During the Job-Interview Process?

Critical. Everything on your application form is vital, but your attitude, the way you view work, is equally significant. Assessing your attitude, of course, is the purpose of the personal interview. Prospective employers hope to pick up a few signals on how you will work with others and handle problems. During an interview you communicate via your attitude as well as with your words. Many employers will hire the positive versus negative interviewee even if the knowledge and skills of the positive person are less impressive.

## Will Learning More about Human Relations Give Me More Self-Confidence When Meeting People for the First Time?

Yes. Without a doubt, the number one reward from a study of human relations is greater confidence. More self-confidence will help you take the first step in meeting others, instead of standing on the sidelines and thinking about it. You will greet your fellow workers pleasantly, even though they might not return the courtesy. You will feel more at ease about communicating with others. And your increased confidence, of course, will greatly help you during the interview process.

## Is a Quiet Person Handicapped When It Comes to Human Relations?

Sometimes. People who tend to be quiet need to make a special effort, especially at the beginning of a new venture. It is difficult to build good relationships with strangers if you back away and refuse to give them a chance to know you.

People who are very quiet or self-sufficient sometimes forget that their silence may be interpreted as aloofness, indifference, or even hostility. To avoid misinterpretation, you should learn to communicate frequently and openly with the people with whom you work. However, it should be encouraging for you to know that many quiet people become highly skilled at human relations later on. The same sensitivity that makes them reserved and reticent also makes them more aware of others' needs.

## Can Good Human Relations Help One Overcome the Handicap of Inexperience?

If you can learn to create and maintain good relationships with all people, young and old and including those with much more experience than yourself, inexperience need not be much of a handicap. One way to gain experience is to respect other people's experience and to learn as much as possible from them. Keep in mind, too, you may have frequent contact with all types of people who have invaluable experience. Always have an open mind toward expanding your knowledge base and developing good relationships. The building of such relationships will test your human-relations skills.

## Why Is It That Some Sophisticated Capable Employees— Even Managers—Seem to Ignore Good Human Relations?

It is difficult to understand. Perhaps some assume that they already practice good human relations, that the subject is too elementary, or that hard work and the work product are all that count. Perhaps they permit the pressures of their jobs to push human relations to the bottom of their priority list. They do not realize that when they let this happen, they stall their career progress.

## Can One Become Competent in Human Relations the Same Way One Can Become Competent as a Computer Operator, Mechanic, or Technician?

In a way, "yes." It is far more difficult, however, to measure human-relations skills. Nevertheless, people will react in a positive way when you practice good human relations and in a negative way when you don't. So your human-relations skills will be observed, even if they can't be measured precisely. (A list of human-relations competencies is presented on the inside of this book's front and back covers.)

## Will Paying More Attention to Human Relations Give One a Brighter Future?

In general, management experts agree that those who concentrate on good human relations get the best jobs and eventually rise to the top in most organizations. Those who pay little attention to human relations seem to get lost and are pushed into the least desirable jobs. All organizations are built around people. And when you build healthy relationships with your fellow workers and supervisors, you open doors that would otherwise be closed.

Look at it this way. You have energy; you have high potential; you have the desire to succeed. All of this is great, but you can't put it to work unless you work well with people—because people, if they want to, can put up roadblocks at every corner. Whether you accept it or not, people will control your job future, and the better the relationships you build with them, the better things will be for you.

## Why Is Human Relations More Important Today Than It Was Thirty or Forty Years Ago?

There are many reasons. Here are five of the most important ones:

1. In previous years, more employees worked alone and therefore did not have to concern themselves with the interpersonal relationships that are necessary to achieve high standards of excellence in a modern business enterprise.

2. Today more workers are employed in service occupations where the future of the organization depends on how well the customer is served. Customer service makes human relations more important throughout the company.

3. Higher productivity among employees is the key to improved profit and an increase in the standard of living for all people. In order to build superior work teams, employees need greater competence in human-relations skills.

4. More and more supervisors are being trained in human relations. Training can cause a supervisor to set higher human-relations standards and to expect greater human-relations efforts from all employees.

5. The modern work force is composed of a more varied mix of personalities and cultures. Thus, the necessity—and challenge—of building strong human relations with all kinds of people is greater.

## Is Human Relations as Important in Small Organizations as It Is in Large Ones?

"Yes." There are some important differences, though, between functioning in large and small organizations. Your progress over the long run may depend more on good human relations in a large company than in a small company. Why? Because there is more supervision and more human-relations responsibility in a large company. Some higher positions in these organizations are almost exclusively leadership positions, where human relations is 60 or 70 percent of the total job.

Also, the big companies were the first to introduce human-relations training for supervisors. They are likely to place more importance on it. It follows that because smaller companies may not provide as much training and assistance, you may have to develop human-relations skills on your own.

## Will Becoming Competent in Human Relations Help One Become a Better Supervisor or Team Leader?

Emphatically, "yes." Not only will you become a better supervisor or team leader, you will become one sooner. The degree to which you develop your human-relations skills now will strongly influence your progress later. Of course, other factors, such as your willingness to work, also play an important role. But the daily application of the techniques you learn through this book will unquestionably have something to do with the pace of your progress. The last chapter in this book addresses this subject.

## Are Extroverted People Automatically Good at Human Relations?

Not necessarily. Human relations is sensitivity to others. Extroverted people are often too concerned with themselves to be good at building relationships with others. The skills and principles outlined in this book can be learned and applied by both extroverts and introverts.

## Why Are Some People So Obviously Awkward at Human Relations?

That's a tough question because each personality is different. Here are a few possibilities. Some individuals are so self-centered that they think only of themselves and therefore give little consideration to the feelings of others. Some are blinded by ambition to the point where they seriously jeopardize their relationships with others. Still others let their emotions spill over at the wrong time, destroying relationships they have carefully built. It may be hard to admit, but we all make mistakes in building and maintaining relationships with people. None of us will ever be perfect, but we should never stop trying to improve.

## Does High Academic Performance Guarantee High Performance on the Job?

No. An individual can be outstanding academically but very weak in human-relations skills. The work environment is different, people are different, and the objectives in business are different from those in the classroom. It is frequently true that a student who is average in the classroom is outstanding on the job, and vice versa. Thus, some students who are high achievers academically might have more of an adjustment to make to the world of work than those who get more practical experience along the way.

## Is There a Relationship between Attitude and Learning?

Yes. The expression "openness to learning" is used to communicate that when a mind is open (free of blocks, fears, prejudices, hang-ups), it will more readily accept and retain new data and ideas. For example, if a student dreads taking a required course (calculus, chemistry, English, etc.), the chances of success are diminished because the fear constitutes a block to learning. However, through an "attitude adjustment" counseling session with the instructor, the block may be partially eliminated. Learning will be easier because the student's attitude is more positive toward learning.

## Must One Change One's Personality to Become Better at Human Relations?

You are what you are, and you cannot become someone else. However, you can change many of your habits, attitudes, and behaviors in working with people. You can develop the personality you already have by becoming more effective in human relationships.

## What Is the Connection between Attitude and Personality?

There is a symbiotic relationship between the two. Personality is generally considered to be the sum total of special physical and mental characteristics that allow you to transmit a unique image to others. The special blend that comes through constitutes your personality. When your positive attitude is in charge, the image communicated is at its best.

You may be proud of one or more of your physical characteristics (eyes, posture, smile, etc.). The same may be true of mental traits (ability to learn, patience, determination, etc.). Attitude, however, is the only characteristic that transcends other traits and pulls them together into a more attractive image. The magic of a positive attitude is that it has a way of making your eyes sparkle more brightly, causing your smile to be more engaging and generally improving your total countenance.

Your positive attitude can best be viewed as a background "light" that enhances your other characteristics. When you are positive, the traits you desire to feature come to life. They are highlighted. Even your less favorable traits appear more attractive. Your total personality is appreciated and enjoyed more by others.

## What Is Charisma?

Charisma is a special blend of a few physical and mental characteristics that seem to communicate a touch of magic. To most people, President John F. Kennedy had charisma. Many movie stars have it. Most of us do not have recognizable charisma. But when we have a positive attitude, we come close. And even those individuals who have charisma usually lose it if they don't keep positive attitudes.

## Do Some People Needlessly Carry Around a Poor Image?

Unfortunately, "yes." Carrying around a poor image can be very damaging because it places a person at a real disadvantage for building relationships. A poor image also leads to a negative attitude. On the other hand, a good image of yourself promotes a positive attitude and brings your best traits to the surface.

## Will This Book Really Help Me Become Human Relations Competent?

If you give it a try, "yes." Your biggest job, of course, will be to apply what you learn in this book to your present job and in your personal life. If you practice a technique long enough, it becomes a habit and you do it automatically. It won't be easy, though, because no one is ever human-relations perfect. Your goal is not to become perfect but to become substantially more effective. Practicing good human relations will make the difference you need to become successful.

> *Can you afford to resist adjusting when change is the only constant in life?*

# Case 2

**"Don't ask me . . . I just work here."**

# Adjustment

Ann and George were both young, aggressive, and competent information systems specialists. They met during a training program in preparation for identical jobs involving considerable contact with fellow employees.

Although it was not easy, Ann made a good adjustment to her work environment. Adjusting was easy for her because of her warm, flexible personality. She also applied the human-relations skills she had learned and developed in college. George, on the other hand, had some difficulty with his assignment. He appeared to be rigid and distant to those who worked around him. To a few older and experienced employees, he even seemed aloof and hostile. George's supervisor watched him from a distance. The supervisor felt George waited or expected others to approach him and be friendly. George seemed to stand on the sidelines, unable or unwilling to initiate interaction or communication, let alone to meet people halfway.

A few weeks after joining the company, George told Ann during lunch he was going to look for another job. When asked why, he said some co-workers were unfriendly. He also resented some of his fellow employees who were excessively critical of him. Furthermore, his supervisor was trying to push him into a mold of conformity that was simply not his style. Why should he go all out to adjust? After all, building working relationships should be a two-way street. He felt confident he could find another company that would appreciate him more and give him all the freedom he needed to be himself.

What chance do you think George has of finding a job environment that would make him completely happy? Assume that you are George's supervisor and are willing to spend thirty minutes in a two-way communication session trying to help him and keep him with the firm. What points would you attempt to cover? (For a suggested answer, see page 225.)

# Hold On to Your Positive Attitude

**"It's hard to stay positive under pressure."**

Thought for the Day: If your attitude has thorns, you cannot expect others to want to get close to you.

*Attitude* is a common word. You hear it almost every day. Professors use it on campus. Managers discuss it at work. Employment counselors look for it among applicants. You hear people say: "He's got an attitude" (indicating a possible problem), while others say "I wish I had her consistently positive attitude." No other attribute will have more influence upon your future. A positive attitude can be your most priceless possession.

If you can create and keep a positive attitude toward your job, your company, and life in general, you should not only move up the ladder of success quickly and gracefully, you should also be a happier person. If you are unable to be positive, you may find many career mobility doors closed to you, and your personal life less than exciting.

## Three Faces of Communication

There are three forms of communication between people. One is the written form—letters, memos, faxes, e-mails, etc. The second is the verbal form—face-to-face conversations, telephone conversations, voice mail, intercom discussions, video conferencing, etc. The third involves the transmission of attitudes.

The first two forms of communication are so important to the profitable operation of an organization that we tend to think they are the only ones. We forget that we also communicate our attitudes through facial expressions, hand gestures, and other more subtle forms of body language. Sometimes people will greet others with a positive voice, but their body language (negative facial expression) sends a contrasting signal. As the expression claims, sometimes your attitude speaks so loudly that others cannot hear what you say.

## Your Attitude Is Showing

Every time you report for work, every time you attend a staff meeting, every time you go through a formal appraisal, every time you take a coffee break, and every time you go out socially, be aware that *your attitude is showing.*

Because attitude can play such an important role in your future, let's take a closer look at the meaning of the word itself. *Attitude* is defined by most psychologists as a mental set that causes a person to respond in a characteristic manner to a given stimulus. You have many attitudes, or mental sets. You have attitudes toward certain makes of automobiles, toward certain social institutions (schools, churches, and the like), toward certain careers, lifestyles, and people.

You also have a wide variety of job attitudes. You build attitudes toward your supervisor and the people with whom you work, toward the job you do, toward company policies, toward the amount of money you are being paid. In addition to these specific attitudes, you have a basic, or total, attitude toward your job and toward life itself. Strictly speaking, then, attitude is the *way you look at your whole environment.*

You can look at your job in any way you wish. On the one hand, you can focus your attention on all its negative aspects (odd hours, close supervision, poor location). On the other hand, you can focus your attention on the more positive factors of the job (harmonious work environment, good learning opportunities, good benefits). All jobs have both positive and negative factors. How you choose to perceive yours is an important decision.

Attitude is the way you view and interpret your environment. Some people can push unpleasant things out of sight and dwell largely on positive factors. Others seem to enjoy the unpleasant and dwell on these negative factors.

## What You See in Life Influences Your Attitude

If you go around looking for what is wrong with things, wondering why things are not better, and complaining about them, then you will be a negative person in the minds of most people. If you do the opposite—look for what is good and focus on pleasant things—you will be a positive person in the minds of most people.

Some people (through imaging) keep their positive attitudes by viewing life as a circle with both positive and negative factors competing to gain as much "mind time" as possible. Negative factors constantly try to command attention, pushing positive factors to the side.

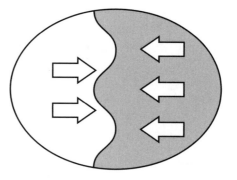

To offset a negative drift, positive people discipline their minds to concentrate primarily upon positive factors, thus pushing the negative to the outer perimeter of their thinking.

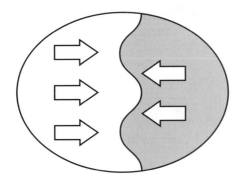

There is no perfect job or position. One job may have more favorable aspects than another, but all jobs have some unpleasant ones. The employee who dwells on the unfavorable factors has a negative attitude. The employee who is determined to look for factors that are favorable will slowly become a more positive person.

Therefore, even if you start a new job or assignment with a positive attitude, you must make sure that it remains positive. It is possible that you will meet a few people with negative attitudes who will attempt to persuade you to think as they do. These factors could influence you and destroy what otherwise would have been an excellent start.

To be a positive person, you need not think your world or company is perfect. That would be foolish. You would eventually become disillusioned. On the other hand, unless you feel that the majority of factors are favorable, you will eventually become negative, and you will show it.

## The Moment You Can No Longer Be Positive about Your Career with Your Company, Your Chances for Success Diminish

No one can be positive all the time. You will naturally have periods of doubt. These temporary periods will not hurt you seriously. But a consistently negative attitude that persists for weeks or months will destroy your future with the organization. If you find your negative attitude cannot be improved in your present setting, and you honestly feel such an attitude is justified, you should resign.

A positive attitude is essential to career success for many reasons:

1. When you are positive you are usually more energetic, motivated, productive, and alert. Thinking about negative things too much has a way of draining your energy. Put another way, a positive attitude opens a gate and lets your inner enthusiasm spill out. A negative attitude, on the other hand, will keep the gate closed.

2. First impressions are important on the job because they often have a lasting effect. Co-workers you meet for the first time appear to have little radar sets tuned in to your attitude. If your attitude is positive, they receive a friendly, warm signal, and they are attracted to you. If your attitude is negative, they receive an unfriendly signal, and they try to avoid you.

3. A positive employee contributes to the productivity of others. A negative employee does not. Attitudes are caught more than they are taught. Both negative and positive attitudes are transmitted on the job. They are picked up by others. A persistently negative attitude, like the rotten apple in the barrel, can spoil the positive attitudes of others. It is very difficult to maintain a high level of productivity while working next to a person with a negative attitude.

4. Co-workers like you when you are positive. They like to be around you because you are fun. Your job is more interesting and exciting because you are in the middle of things and not on the outside complaining. When you are negative, people prefer to stay clear of you. A negative person may build good relationships with a few other people (who are perhaps negative themselves), but such a person cannot build good relationships with the majority of employees.

5. The kind of attitude you transmit to management will have a considerable influence on your future success. Management constantly reads your mental attitude, even though you may feel you are successful in covering it up. Supervisors can determine your attitude by how you approach your job, react to directives, handle problems, and work with others. If you are positive, you will be given greater consideration when special assignments and promotion opportunities arise.

If your job involves customer, client, or patient contacts, you should place additional emphasis on everything stated in the preceding list. Your attitude is significant in all relationships, but it is crucial when you are in a service position.

It is important to realize that a positive attitude involves far more than a smile. A smile, of course, is helpful in transmitting a positive attitude. However, some people transmit a positive attitude even when they seldom smile. They convey positiveness by the way they treat others, the way they look at their responsibilities, and the perspective they take when faced with a problem.

Attitude is a highly personal thing. It is closely tied to your self-concept, or the way you look at yourself. Because attitude is so personal, talking about it is not easy. People often freeze when the word is mentioned. As a result, management may never talk to you about your attitude. They may never say, for example, "Let's be honest. Your attitude is negative. What are you going to do about it?" *But everyone will know when your attitude is showing.*

How, then, do you make sure you keep your positive attitude when things get tough? How do you keep a good grip on it when you are discouraged? How do you keep it in good repair on a day-to-day basis over the years? Here are a few simple suggestions.

## Build a More Positive Attitude in One Environment and You Will Be More Successful in Another

Your positive or negative attitude is not something that you can hang on a hook. It follows you wherever you go. It is reasonable to assume, then, that if you make a greater effort to be a more positive person in your social and personal lives, your effort will automatically spill over and help you on the job. By the same token, if you make a greater effort to develop a more positive attitude at work, your effort will make a contribution to your social and personal lives. One effort will complement the other.

## Talk about Positive Things

Negative comments are seldom welcomed by fellow workers on the job; nor are they welcomed by those you meet in the social scene. The best way to be positive is to be complimentary. Constant gripers and complainers seldom build healthy and exciting relationships with others.

## Look For the Good Things in the People with Whom You Work, Especially Your Supervisors

Nobody is perfect, but almost everybody has a few worthwhile qualities. If you dwell on people's good features, it will be easier for you to like them and easier for them to like you. Make no mistake about one thing: People usually know how you react to them even if you don't communicate verbally.

## Look For the Good Things in Your Organization

What are the factors that make it a good place to work? Do you like the hours, the physical environment, the people, the actual work you are doing? What about opportunities for promotion? Do you have chances for self-improvement? What about your wage and benefit package? Do you have the freedom you seek? No job is perfect, but, if you concentrate on the good things, the negative factors may seem less important. Seeing the positive side of things does not mean that you should ignore negative elements that should be changed. Far from it! A positive person is not a weak person. A positive person is usually confident, assertive (within limits), and an agent of change within an organization. Management is not seeking passive people who meekly conform. They want spirited, positive people who will make constructive and thoughtful improvements.

If you decide to stay with an organization for a long time, you would be wise to concentrate on its good features. Staying positive may take a considerable amount of personal fortitude, but it is the best way to keep your career on an upward track. If you think positively, you will act positively and you will succeed.

## Avoid Financial Problems through Planning and Discipline

On-campus surveys indicate that students frequently fail academically and drop out because of financial problems. It also appears that career employees troubled with financial worries often turn negative and lose the promotions that would provide the extra money that could help them pay off their bills. Unfortunately, few of these individuals realize that their positive attitudes are being sacrificed along with their credit ratings. Instead of seeking and accepting family or professional financial counseling, they permit their insolvency to lead them into attitudinal bankruptcy. When attitudinal bankruptcy happens, they pay a double penalty.

## Don't Permit a Fellow Worker—Even a Supervisor—Who Has a Negative Attitude to Trap You into His (or Her) Way of Thinking

You may not be able to change a negative person's attitude, but at least you can protect your own positive attitude from becoming negative. The story of Sandy will emphasize this point.

> **Sandy.** Sandy was a little uneasy about her new job. It was a fine opportunity, and she knew the standards were very high. Would she have the skills needed? Could she learn fast enough to please her supervisor? Would the older employees like her? Although Sandy's concern was understandable, it was not justified. In addition to being highly qualified for the job, she had a happy, positive attitude that wouldn't stop. She was seldom depressed.
>
> Everything went very well for Sandy for a while. Her positive attitude was appreciated by all. Slowly, however, her fellow workers and supervisor noticed a change. Sandy became more critical of her colleagues, her job, and the company. Her usual friendly greetings and helpful ideas were gradually replaced by complaints. What had happened? Without realizing it, Sandy was showing the effects of the friendships she had made on the job. Needing acceptance in a strange environment, she had welcomed the attention of a clique of employees who had a negative attitude—a group that management already viewed critically.

Sandy was not able to confine her negative attitude to her job. Soon, again without realizing it, she let her negative attitude spill over into her social life. In fact, it troubled her boyfriend so much that he had it out with her one night. His words were a little rough. "Look, Sandy. When you are happy, you are very attractive and fun to be around. But frankly, when you are negative you are a real bore, and I never have a good time with you. I think those so-called friends you hang round with on the job are killing what was once a beautiful personality."

It wasn't a happy evening, but Sandy got the message. She made a vow to recapture and hang on to the positive attitude she had previously enjoyed. Not only was she successful in recapturing her positive attitude, but she also converted a few of her previously negative friends to her way of thinking. Her action saved her career.

## Make Frequent Self-Assessments

When friends casually ask me "How are you doing?" I often jokingly reply: "I'm not sure but I intend to sit under a tree tomorrow and ask myself some questions to find out." Most employees make the mistake of waiting around for their organizations to complete an annual formal appraisal instead of frequently sitting under a shady tree somewhere and asking themselves questions similar to these.

Am I currently transmitting a positive or negative attitude?

Is my attitude influencing the quality and quantity of my personal productivity in a positive way?

Am I sufficiently positive to be considered a fun and comfortable co-worker?

Am I communicating to superiors through my attitude that I seek career advancements?

Are my customers, clients, or co-workers responding to my attitude in an upbeat manner?

Whatever form your self-assessment takes (attitude is a most personal matter), *use it frequently.* Check your attitude as you would the amount of gasoline in your car. Talk to yourself about the progress you are making. Don't sit around expecting someone else to do it for you.

**John.** John's boss is a believer in formal appraisal programs. Instead of annual evaluations, he would prefer going through the process twice each year. In discussing the good showing John made on his current appraisal, his boss said: "John, I have noticed that your attitude and productivity always improves shortly before appraisal time and then settles back a few weeks afterward. I think it would be smart for you to appraise yourself every few weeks during the year. By periodic appraisal checks you would keep a more positive attitude and deserve a higher rating than I can give you now. Consistency is a big factor and I recommend frequent self-appraisals."

## Serendipity

Holding on to your positive attitude will never be easy. There are many techniques, however, that can help. Some will be discussed later in this book. One that will help you get started, especially when an irritating problem surfaces, is saying the word *serendipity.*

The word *serendipity* was coined by Horace Walpole in 1754 when he put the fairy tale *The Three Princes of Serendip* to paper. A modern version by Elizabeth Jamison Hodges was published in 1964. It is a delightful story of three princes who travel from kingdom to kingdom in a lighthearted, compassionate manner. In helping others solve their problems, they are led to the solution of a problem in their own kingdom.

Serendipity lends itself to many interpretations. To some, it is a gift to help them find agreeable things not sought. To everyone it is a "happiness" word. The magic comes into play when we realize that a "lighter approach" can often not only solve a problem but cause something good to happen in our lives.

In short, serendipity is an attitude—an apparently frivolous mental set that can help us view our work environment in a more humorous and forgiving manner. It is an attitude that temporarily moves responsibility aside and encourages one to rise above any negative situation. A serendipitous attitude is within the reach of everyone and, when achieved, fortuitous things may happen. For example, when you have a lighthearted, mischievous, festive way of looking at things, others are intrigued and may invite you to share beautiful experiences with them that, in turn, can enhance your life. Serendipity is a state of mind. It is a wonderful attitude to take to a party. There are also times when it can be a lifesaver in the workplace.

> *Like plants, your attitude needs nurturing in order to grow.*

# Case 3

**"Financial solvency helps keep my attitude positive."**

# Credit Blues

Manuel, a graphics artist with multi-media skills, was constantly praised by his college professors for his creative works. He was also rewarded by winning a number of prizes in campus art shows. Upon graduating, Manuel made many attempts to find a job in commercial art. No luck. After many disappointments, he reluctantly accepted a position with a large retail chain that would have only limited use for his talent in the area of merchandising display.

Manuel decided to make the most of his situation and began his career with a positive attitude. He quickly demonstrated that he had both talent and managerial ability. His future looked bright. He was happy. Some time later, however, his supervisor noticed that Manuel's enthusiasm had started to dwindle. He began giving excuses for not getting things done on time. Manuel's merchandise displays were not up to previous standards. His relationships with other workers started to deteriorate.

In a heart-to-heart talk with his sensitive and supportive manager, Manuel revealed that he was having serious financial problems. Manuel's quest for finding satisfying challenges had led him to obsessive and impulsive Internet shopping and stock trading. As it took more and more stimuli to satisfy his "needs," Manuel's acquisitions and debts grew too. Through the purchase of a new sports car and other consumer items, Manuel was behind on his credit payments, and the high interest rates were keeping him in the hole. Manuel's manager told him he was suffering from a severe case of "plastic blues" and sent him to a company counselor with expertise in financial planning.

Would you agree that financial problems can damage a positive attitude and derail one's career? What suggestions would you give to Manuel to help him stay positive while he digs himself out of his financial hole? (For a suggested answer, see page 225.)

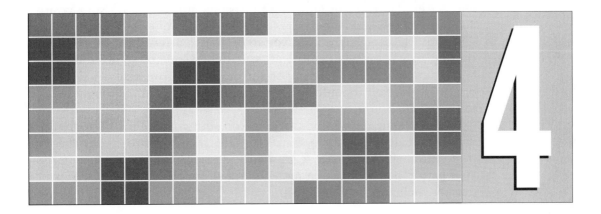

# When People Step on Your Attitude

**"Another day on the job!"**

Thought for the Day: Adjusting your attitude in a positive direction—and often—will only improve it.

On a given day, three or four different people might step on your positive attitude and render you negative for a short period of time. For example, an insensitive teacher might press you to deliver an answer to a difficult question in such a way as to embarrass you; or someone in your family might back away from keeping an important promise you were depending upon; or a co-worker you thought was your friend might "snub" you in an off-the-job social environment.

Even in simple situations, stepping on your attitude is like stepping on your ego. It deflates your personal confidence and destroys your effectiveness. Although the damage to your attitude may be slight, it takes effort on your part to bounce back. In more serious situations bouncing back can be a major challenge.

> **Gregg.** About a month ago Gregg missed what appeared to be a "sure" tackle in a key college football game. Furious, his coach pulled him out of the game and chewed him out in front of others. The verbal lacing hit Gregg's attitude so hard that he was tempted to turn in his equipment. "After all," Gregg told his teammates, "the turf was wet and I slipped. It could have happened to anyone." With encouragement from others, however, he discussed the incident with his coach, pumped up his depressed attitude, and finished the season at such a high level that he kept his athletic scholarship.

> **Jennifer.** Last week, due to a misunderstanding, Jennifer got into a conflict with her boss and emotionally unloaded some stored-up grievances. Her boss, Ms. Bailey, came down on her hard. Rather than attempt to resolve the problem so she could keep and enjoy her part-time job again, Jennifer nursed her grievance, which kept her positive attitude from bouncing back. Result? She was given notice and quickly discovered that she had walked away from a job that was better than any she could find.

> **Jill and Roberto.** Having been married almost a year, it became obvious that things were not going to work out for Jill and Roberto. After the separation process was under way, it was also obvious that Jill was allowing the whole matter to get under her skin. Roberto's outward acceptance of the separation, the legal conferences with the lawyers, and the breaking up of their apartment all combined to step on Jill's attitude in a devastating manner. She finally went to her older sister for guidance. Her sister made this statement: "Face it, Jill, your attitude has taken a beating and bouncing back is a do-it-yourself project. Don't you think it is time to get started? I will do everything I can to help."

Human conflicts both on the job and in our personal lives can turn our attitudes negative. The damage can sometimes be severe. But if such conflicts are permitted to destroy our positive attitudes on a permanent basis, we are paying a price that is much too high. What can we do to "bounce back"? What can we do to restore our positive attitudes? Here are some suggestions.

# Take Immediate Action

It is a mistake to wait around and "nurse" your deflated attitude. Quickly do something to restore it so that additional damage will not occur. In some cases this may mean an apology that you don't want to make.

> **Ralph.** Yesterday Ralph made a foolish mistake that could have been minimized if he had reported it to his boss immediately. However, before Ralph could offer his boss an explanation, an insensitive co-worker stepped on Ralph's attitude. Ralph became so upset with getting his attitude stepped on, he forgot to report the mistake to his boss. Not reporting the mistake caused Ralph to have a poor night's sleep. To restore his attitude, Ralph got to work early the next morning and apologized to his boss. Ralph was in full possession of his positive attitude by noon.

Generally speaking, the longer you allow your attitude to be depressed, the longer it takes to bounce back. Quick action, even if it is embarrassing, is advisable.

# Place a Higher Value on Your Positive Attitude

The more you respect and covet your positive attitude, the more you will want to take quick action to preserve it. Normally, we only protect those possessions that we deem priceless. When you come to the conclusion your positive attitude is the golden key to your future, you will want to restore it as soon as possible once it has been stepped on.

> **Genelle.** Some co-workers pile extra, uninteresting work on Genelle because she has the reputation of being so easy-going. When she belatedly discovered that being such a "push-over" around the office was turning her negative, she did an about face and, as a result, she is respected more and fewer co-workers step on her attitude these days.

# Learn to See Both Sides of Situations

Sometimes a friend or coworker may step on your attitude because she (or he) is under pressure and is rendered insensitive to your needs. When this happens, you have two choices. You can allow your attitude to remain depressed and become the victim. Or you can give the other party the benefit of the doubt and restore your attitude to its normal positive stance without making a major issue out of what happened.

> **Sylvia.** Immediately Sylvia knew her attitude had been stepped on when her co-worker didn't show up at the appointed location and was seen later with another person. What Sylvia didn't know was that there had been a family emergency and the co-worker was headed for the hospital with her

sister. When she arrived at work the next morning, her friend was waiting to explain what had happened. Sylvia could feel her positive attitude returning before the discussion had ended.

## Protect Yourself So It Won't Happen Twice

Some people will step on your attitude once and, if they get away with it, will step on it again. The behavior of some people is such that they are either insensitive to your needs or they do not give you the respect you deserve. Some supervisors are this way. Some family members or co-workers are this way. In these situations you need to protect your attitude by standing up for yourself, isolating yourself from the individual, or using other techniques to open up a two-way discussion with this person so that you and your attitude will be treated with respect and sensitivity.

> **Hank.** Hank's boss kept stepping on his attitude by making unkind snide remarks, giving him undesirable assignments, and generally treating him like a second-class employee. Finally, Hank asked for a private appointment and confronted his boss with the question: "Am I not entitled to the same kind of treatment as my co-workers?" Hank's boss replied: "I was only testing you. You have now made the grade, so we will have a different kind of relationship from now on."

## Avoid Putting Other People Down

If you expect people to respect you and be sensitive to your needs, don't step on other peoples' attitudes. One of the best ways you can keep your attitude from being stepped on is making sure you give other people the same consideration you expect. Value and respect the views, perspectives, and feelings of others. There is always more than one side to an issue and more than one way to solve a problem. It may take more effort on your part to avoid stepping on another person's attitude, but it will be worth it in the long run. You will increase your sensitivity to plausible alternatives, and you will get to know people better. As a result you will be able to get your ideas across more effectively. It is vital to watch and listen to others for a better understanding of their perspectives. Be sure you seek this type of feedback to assure you truly are communicating.

> **Steve.** Frequently Steve played the "one upmanship" game by building himself up in front of groups of people. One-on-one he would be very careful not to give out too much information. But in a meeting it was a different story. When an issue was discussed in a group setting, Steve was very quiet until near the end of the discussion when he would give his opinion. His opinion always seemed to be the way the "wind was blowing" by his supervisor. He was so good at rephrasing others' views, the key point he

made frequently could solve the problem. His co-workers, however, felt his comments were offered at their expense. He took great pride in his ability to make people understand "he was the only one who had complete information" or that "he should always be consulted."

If you consider your attitude to be your most priceless possession, as many people do, you cannot—under any circumstances—permit others to turn it negative. When they knowingly or unknowingly step on your positive attitude, you must resort to whatever technique is comfortable and appropriate to restore it. If you do not quickly restore your attitude, you are, in effect, allowing a person to "take" or "steal" your positive attitude from you.

Should someone try to damage your positive attitude, keep in mind that your attitude belongs to you alone. It cannot be given or transferred to another person. It is not negotiable. You have the right to protect your positive attitude from anyone who might damage it over an extended period of time. It is one thing to have another person step on your attitude unknowingly and then apologize or make amends in other ways. In these situations, you can bounce back quickly and no harm is done. It is another thing altogether when someone steps on your attitude over and over again. Should this happen, action on your part to build a more mutually rewarding relationship is suggested.

Without question, you must bounce back and be the positive person that you are! Here are some important things to remember toward building a strong positive attitude:

1. In one way or another, we all get our attitudes stepped on from time to time. When we bounce back quickly, no harm is done.

2. Bouncing back quickly is not always easy. Sometimes the utilization of certain techniques is necessary to speed up the process.

3. Respect the ideas of other people. If you learn this important rule, you will frequently find your good ideas will become even better and your attitude won't get in the way to solve problems.

4. Your positive attitude is a priceless possession and belongs only to you. Keeping it positive may be your greatest challenge in life.

> *If your attitude needs surgery,*
> *don't expect a vitamin to cure*
> *the ill.*

## Case 4

**"I recover quickly."**

# Bounce Back

Sue Ellen is a physical therapist for a sports medicine clinic in a prestigious hospital. She is highly disciplined, has outstanding work skills, and is quietly effective. Sue Ellen's only problem is that she is super-sensitive to comments and actions from others. She lets her attitude get stepped on and is too easily hurt by people. Sue Ellen is particularly vulnerable to any strong demands from doctors, supervisors, and even patients. When anyone comes down hard or steps on Sue Ellen's attitude, she has a difficult time bouncing back. It's now quite noticeable that Sue Ellen's personal productivity and interaction with people are lowered whenever she gets "down" on herself.

From time to time, Frank, a male nurse in the clinic, is Sue Ellen's immediate supervisor. Frank is well aware of Sue Ellen's sensitivity to demands of others. In fact, on more than one occasion and with increasing frequency, Frank has unavoidably stepped on Sue Ellen's attitude to the point that she has had to step away for a few moments to gain her composure. Frank has never had a heart-to-heart talk with Sue Ellen about why she is so sensitive and why it appears so easy for people to step on her attitude. In recent weeks, Frank feels that Sue Ellen is retreating and, as a result, becoming even more sensitive. Frank has decided there is no time like the present to try to help Sue Ellen become a stronger person so that, regardless of what people say, they do not psychologically step on her attitude.

Even though Frank supervises Sue Ellen only "from time to time," why should he try to help her? How should Frank go about trying to address Sue Ellen's sensitivity problem? What should he say and do to help her? To compare your answer with that of the authors, turn to page 226.

You have now completed Part I of this book. Part I was designed to help you understand yourself and especially the potential of your positive attitude. Part II will introduce you to ways you can use your positive attitude to build and maintain better human relations.

Before going on to Part II of this book, you may want to go back to the beginning of each chapter and think about each of the opening "thought-for-the-day" statements. Also, go to the end of each chapter and read the thoughts provided in each "attitude box." The ideas presented at the start of each chapter and in the attitude boxes were designed for you to ponder and contemplate as you begin assessing your attitude—and making changes toward becoming a more positive person.

# PART II

# Relationships with Others

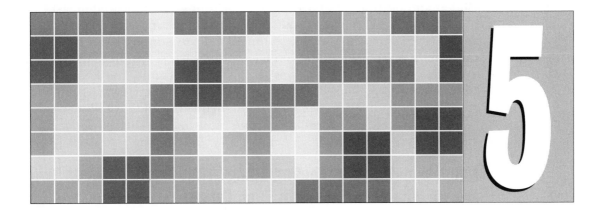

# Vertical and Horizontal Working Relationships

**"Relationships are *that* important?"**

Thought for the Day: Become the kind of person YOU value as a friend or colleague.

Understanding yourself and the power of your positive attitude makes it much easier to meet new people and establish meaningful relationships with them. For example, when you meet a supervisor or co-worker for the first time, a psychological reaction takes place: each person instantaneously interprets the other. It is a feeling that is hard to define. You know something is happening, but you can't put your finger on it. Slowly, as you and the other individual see each other more frequently and get to know each other better, these initial feelings mature into what is called a *relationship*.

## A Relationship Is a "Feeling Thing" That Exists between Two People Who Associate with Each Other

You can't see, taste, smell, or touch a relationship; you can only feel it in a psychological sense. Job relationships are usually different from social relationships. Job relationships exist only because you selected a certain company and were assigned to work with certain people in a specific department. In other words, in your social life you have a choice; on the job you do not. Nevertheless, working relationships are extremely important to you and your future because they will have a strong influence on your personality and personal productivity.

Working relationships of this nature are fascinating to study. For example, one interesting characteristic is that two persons cannot meet regularly on the job or work in the same general areas without having a relationship. So the first thing to learn about working relationships is, whether you like it or not, a relationship will exist between you and every employee or supervisor with whom you have regular contact. While you need not work next to this person, speak to this person, nor even have a desire to know this person, a relationship will still exist.

There appears to be no way to neutralize a relationship under these conditions. The very fact that you might decide to ignore a person does not destroy the relationship; in fact, the opposite may happen. The relationship may become more tense and psychologically powerful. Let us take a specific example.

You notice Francine, an employee working in a department next to you. In an attempt to be friendly, you say hello in a very pleasant way to this person the first day on the job, and you receive no reply.

Does this mean that the relationship is cut off at this point?

Far from it! You may feel that Francine's failure to reply is slighting you, and this may naturally disturb you. You may decide not to take the initiative again. Nevertheless, you will remember this person clearly and wonder what will happen in the future.

The person to whom you said hello, on the other hand, has had some kind of reaction to your friendly gesture. She may feel that she treated you in an unfriendly manner (perhaps she was not feeling well that day) and might welcome another opportunity to be more friendly. Or, she may have interpreted your hello as being a little too forward on your part as a new employee and decided to be cool toward you.

You could ignore her. You could avoid verbal contact. You and she could see each other only a few times a week.

Would a relationship exist?

"Yes," indeed. Two persons have made contact with each other. They see each other occasionally. They work for the same company. As long as these factors exist, a relationship must exist. Under these conditions you cannot erase a relationship. The attempt on the part of one person to withdraw serves only to make the relationship more emotionally charged; it does not in any manner eliminate it.

## You Cannot Consistently Work with or Near People or Communicate with Them Frequently without Having Working Relationships with Them

There is another interesting characteristic about working relationships when viewed objectively. They are either strong or weak, warm or cool, healthy or unhealthy, friendly or distant. There appears to be no absolute neutral ground. Every relationship has a very small positive or negative content.

Have you ever heard someone say, "I can take her or leave her"? The phrase usually means that it doesn't make any difference whether the person referred to is around or not. But the very fact that one makes such a comment indicates that it would be better if the person were not around. The relationship still exists, and in this case it is a little cool.

## Each Relationship You Have Has Its Own Characteristics

Another characteristic of relationships is that each is different. You must build relationships with all kinds of people, regardless of race, religion, age, sex, or personality characteristics. Each relationship will be unique. Each will be built on a different basis. Each will have its own integrity.

As you look around and study your co-workers and your supervisor, you will see that they are all separate personalities. At the same time, your supervisor and co-workers are studying you. Do they all see the same person?

Strange as it may seem, they do not. You do not look the same to different people. You make a different impression on each of them because they interpret you differently.

There is another way of saying this: You do not have a single personality in the eyes of others. Each person interprets you differently, based on his (or her) own unique background, prejudices, likes, dislikes, and so on. Your personality, to that person, is different. The way he interprets your personality is your personality to that person.

Why all this emphasis on the way in which people view your personality? How will this help you become more sensitive to human relationships? Because everybody sees you differently, you will have to build good relationships with different people differently. And make no mistake here. Good relationships must be built. They seldom come about automatically.

## You Will Rarely Build a Strong, Warm, or Healthy Relationship with Two Persons in the Same Way

Because good relationships don't happen by accident and must be consciously built, you will always have to take into consideration the person at the other end of the relationship. To start with, some people are not going to interpret your personality favorably. You are going to have to be sensitive enough to determine who these people are, and then you must build a good relationship with them on an individual basis. It is not easy to change a cool relationship to a warm one, yet you cannot afford to allow it to remain in an unhealthy state. You should make some effort to build it into a stronger relationship. To build a stronger relationship, you should consider the person at the other end of the relationship and remember that she (or he) sees you differently than anyone else.

## Building a Vertical Working Relationship Is a Critical Element of Your Job

A *vertical working relationship* is the relationship between you and your immediate supervisor. If, as a regular employee, you have two or more supervisors, you will have two or more vertical relationships to maintain. Normally, you will have one immediate supervisor, as illustrated here.

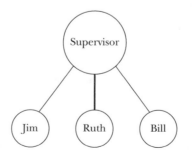

In a small department consisting of one supervisor and three employees, each employee has a different vertical relationship with the same supervisor. This relationship is indicated by the line between each employee and the supervisor, often called the *job relations line*. If the relationship is strong, we indicate this by a heavy line. If it is weak, we indicate the weak relationship by a light line. Naturally it is almost impossible for supervisors to create and maintain an equally strong line between themselves and all the employees in the department. It is their job to try to maintain strong relationships with all workers, and the closer they come to this ideal, the better it is for the department. But supervisors are human beings and are not perfect. Consequently, the job-relations lines are seldom equally strong. The person working next to you might have either a stronger or a weaker relationship with the supervisor than you have.

You will notice in the following illustration that arrows have been added to the lines.

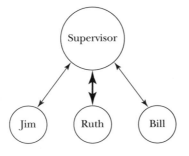

The arrows at the ends of the vertical job-relations lines have real significance. They signify that there should be a free flow of information between the workers and the supervisor. It is extremely difficult for a strong relationship to exist between two persons without two-way communication. The supervisor must feel free to discuss, openly and frankly, certain problems with Ruth, Jim, and Bill. If the supervisor hesitates to talk with Jim about a certain weakness in his job performance, the relationship between the two of them is not what it could be. By the same token, if Jim is hesitant about taking a suggestion or a gripe to the supervisor, the relationship is less than ideal.

## The Lifeblood of a Good Relationship Is Free and Open Communication

Good relationships are built and maintained by free and frequent verbal communication. People need to talk with each other, exchange ideas, voice complaints, and offer suggestions if they intend to keep a good relationship.

The moment that one party refuses to talk things over, the relationship line becomes thin and weak.

The primary responsibility for creating and maintaining a strong vertical relationship rests with the supervisor. Building a vertical relationship line is a responsibility that goes with the position. If the relationship line is in need of repair, it is primarily the supervisor's responsibility to initiate a discussion that can mend the break.

Although the supervisor has the primary responsibility, you as the employee have the secondary responsibility to keep the relationship line strong and healthy. Some employees make the serious mistake of thinking that the supervisor is wholly responsible for making them happy and productive.

Chapter 8 will show you how to create and maintain a good relationship with your supervisor. It suffices now to say that you can't expect the supervisor to do all the relationship building. You will have to work hard to keep a good job-relations line between you and your supervisor. Even if you have an exceptionally poor supervisor, you will have to meet him (or her) halfway. Vertical relationships need to be in healthy repair if departmental productivity is to be high. Often the supervisor finds that it requires considerable tact and delicacy to maintain vertical relationships. Small wonder that management has seen fit to give this person some special training.

## Building a Strong Horizontal Working Relationship Is Another Critical Element of Your Job

Horizontal working relationships are those that exist between you and fellow workers in the same department—the people you work next to on an hour-to-hour, day-to-day basis. The following diagram illustrates the horizontal relationships among three people in a very small department.

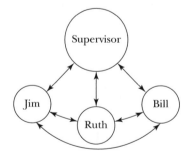

You will note that Jim has a horizontal working relationship with both Ruth and Bill. In this very small department of three employees and one supervisor, Jim has one vertical relationship and two horizontal relationships to keep strong. It is easy to see that in larger departments there would be many more. In fact, the average number of employees in a department is nine.

You (not the supervisor) have the primary responsibility for creating and keeping healthy horizontal relationships. The supervisor—working at a distance in regard to these relationships—has the secondary responsibility. Once in a while she (or he) might find it necessary to step in to help restore a good relationship between two employees. But by and large the supervisor must leave this up to the employees themselves.

The critical need for building good horizontal working relationships is often ignored by some workers. When they reject the need for building good relationships, their doors of opportunity are locked and the keys are thrown away.

It is extremely important to the new employee to build and maintain good horizontal working relationships. In fact, building good relationships should be a major part of your total human-relations effort as you start your career. Much of this book is devoted to the principles and techniques that will assist you in this respect. For example, here are two mistakes you should refrain from making:

1. *Avoid concentrating on building a good relationship with your supervisor and neglecting good relationships with your fellow workers.*

2. *Avoid concentrating on building one or two very strong horizontal working relationships and neglecting those with the remaining fellow workers in your department.*

Making either mistake will cause immediate disharmony in your department and will put you in human-relations hot water. The supervisor cannot afford to have an extremely strong relationship with you and weak relationships with your fellow workers if he (or she) wants high productivity from all. It makes for dissension and immediate cries of favoritism.

From your point of view, then, an overly strong vertical relationship can cause a general weakening of your horizontal working relationships. When you make the mistake of concentrating on one or two horizontal working relationships, the remaining horizontal relationships deteriorate and your vertical relationship with the supervisor is also weakened.

All horizontal working relationships in the same department should be given equal attention and consideration. One should not be strengthened at the expense of others, even though it may be more fun and more satisfying. Balance is important.

When you concentrate on creating good horizontal working relationships with all fellow workers, you almost automatically create a good vertical relationship with your supervisor. It should be recognized, of course, that the success of this principle is assured only if the supervisor is sufficiently sensitive to the working environment. In the majority of cases, work environment sensitivity is a fair assumption. A perceptive supervisor will greatly appreciate any employee who builds a better team spirit in the department by creating and maintaining strong horizontal working relationships.

## Building Good Broad-Based Relationships with as Many People as Possible Should Be a General Goal for You

There are, of course, important relationships other than those indicated in the diagrams. Your relationship-building activity should not be confined to a single department. It is a good idea for you to expand your sphere of influence as quickly as possible on your new job. The more good relationships you build, the better.

As important as peripheral relationships are, they are not your primary working relationships. You cannot afford to concentrate on building relationships outside your department by neglecting those on the inside.

The building of a strong vertical relationship with your immediate supervisor and strong horizontal working relationships with your fellow workers is absolutely essential to your personal success. No other human-relations activity should have a higher priority.

> *Life without continuously working at building good relationships is not living.*

# Case 5

**"My supervisor ignores me."**

# Decision

Bernie, a budding engineer apprentice, was getting used to working with all types of people on project management teams. He seemed to "fit in" wherever he was assigned and built good relationships. Recently, however, because of a realignment of personnel, Bernie was transferred (against his wishes) to the traffic department. In his new assignment he would have to build seven horizontal relationships and one vertical relationship. Bernie was the junior member of the department. All the other employees, including the supervisor, were much older than he.

After one week in the new department, Bernie discovered that it was difficult to approach his supervisor, Gloria, let alone talk to her. Bernie also found that Gloria stayed aloof from the workers in the department and that she often seemed critical of most people. Bernie could feel a psychological barrier between his boss and the rest of the department employees. Once a week Gloria held a short staff meeting. In Bernie's first departmental meeting with Gloria and co-workers, he observed that most of the employees were silent and even seemed somewhat hostile.

How could Bernie build a strong, worthwhile vertical relationship with his boss whose nature was so distant within an environment that was so structured? Wouldn't he be wiser to concentrate exclusively on horizontal relationships until an opportunity presented itself to establish a better relationship with Gloria? After giving the matter some serious thought, Bernie decided to concentrate on horizontal relationships and weather it out.

Was this a smart decision on Bernie's part? Would you have gone about it differently? Support your point of view. (For a suggested answer, see page 226.)

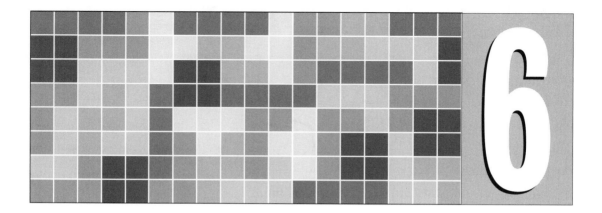

# Productivity—A Closer Look

**"Being productive requires more than technical skills."**

Thought for the Day: Giving your best effort to an endeavor can never be faulted.

A manufacturing plant, in order to be competitive with other operations turning out a similar product, must *produce* at the lowest possible cost per single item or unit. A retail store, in order to pay overhead expenses and show a profit, must *produce* sales at a certain level. An airline must *produce* a reliable service that will attract enough customers to keep the seats filled. Even a municipal organization like a fire department must *produce* at a level that will satisfy taxpayers. Every kind of organization must produce, and when production is not sufficient to make a profit or satisfy people, changes are made. These are economic facts of life.

## Measuring Productivity

Because productivity* is so important, management has devised ways of measuring it. Productivity is easily measured on an assembly line where the worker must perform a specific function, such as connecting a wire or screwing on a nut. Assembly or production line jobs can be time studied and a standard rate established. If the standard rate is eighty-five completions in sixty minutes, it means that the average worker can reach and sustain this number over a certain period of time.

Measurable jobs or tasks of this nature are found primarily in the manufacturing and fabricating industries. Other jobs, such as customer service and office work, are more difficult to measure because factors such as how much initiative is demonstrated, how people are treated, and how the telephone is answered are difficult to measure.

Productivity, then, can be measured scientifically in some situations, but in countless others it can only be measured by management judgment. Regardless of the kind of job you now hold or the way in which your productivity is measured, understanding what is meant by productivity (from the management point of view) is important to your future.

There are two kinds of productivity.

- *Individual productivity.* Individual productivity is the contribution a single person makes to getting the departmental job done. It is the amount of work one person does in comparison with that of others in the group or section. It may or may not be measurable.

- *Group productivity.* Group productivity is the sum total of all individual contributions, including that of the supervisor. It can be—and often is—measured objectively, that is, reduced to figures and statistics.

---

*The reader is reminded that when using the word *productivity*, the authors mean *quality* performance. Management is only interested in producing more products or services when it reaches standards of excellence.

# Individual Productivity Potentials

Each worker has a current (day-to-day, week-to-week) level of productivity that generally remains constant, although it may fluctuate from time to time. Let us illustrate this through the use of a glass or beaker. Assume that the liquid in the glass is the current level of productivity for a person we will call Jane. Like all employees, Jane also has a potential level of productivity that is greater than her current level.

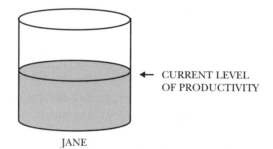

JANE

Seldom, if ever, does a person reach his or her full potential. Jane would be the first to agree with this. So let us draw a dotted line across the glass to indicate Jane's potential level of productivity. We don't know exactly where Jane's potential might be. It is impossible to measure her capacity or potential scientifically because more than her mental ability is involved—and even her mental ability cannot be measured accurately. But for our hypothetical situation, we can say that Jane's potential is somewhat above her current level of productivity.

In the preceding diagram, then, Jane's current level of productivity is indicated by the solid line, and her potential or possible level of productivity is indicated by the dotted line. The difference between the two is what we will call the *productivity gap*.

There is always a gap between what one could do and what one actually does. Of course, management would like to see Jane close the gap be-

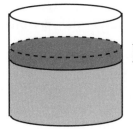

} PRODUCTIVITY GAP

tween her current and potential productivity levels as much as possible, but it would be asking too much to expect her to close it completely.

We are concerned, then, not so much with the gap itself as with the size of the gap. If it is small, Jane's supervisor knows she is working close to her capacity. If it is large, the supervisor knows that something is wrong and should be looked into.

Jane's supervisor should, of course, do all she (or he) can to keep the distance between Jane's potential and her current performance as small as possible. If the gap becomes too great, she might decide that Jane needs additional training, a special incentive, a change in assignment rotation, or perhaps some form of counseling. The supervisor cannot permit Jane's level of productivity to remain substandard over an extended period of time.

Jane, of course, is not the only worker in the department. In our hypothetical situation, let us assume that there are two other employees occupying positions identical to Jane's. These people are Art and Fred.

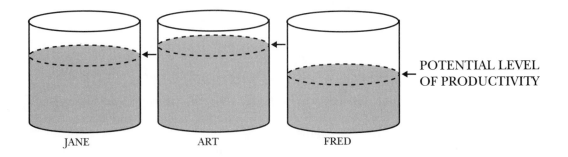

POTENTIAL LEVEL
OF PRODUCTIVITY

JANE          ART          FRED

You will note that the potentials of Art and Fred are different from Jane's. It is somewhat disturbing at first to recognize that everyone has a different potential and that some people have higher potentials than others. However, potential variability is in fact true because everyone differs in mental ability (IQ), ability to endure physical strain (stamina and endurance), ability to perform certain manipulative skills (dexterity), creative level, inner drive, and attitude, as well as in other personality characteristics. All these features together make up an individual's potential.

It is important not to get hung up over the word *potential*. As we are using it, potential simply means the level of productivity a worker might achieve under ideal circumstances if he (or she) pushed himself to his limit. It is seldom, if ever, reached. In using the word *potential* however, we should remember that some employees are outstanding in some areas and average or below in others. Few, if any, are outstanding in all areas. Yet, almost everyone has at least one exceptional characteristic.

We need not be concerned about the measurement of potential. (In fact, there is no truly scientific way to measure it.) All that we need be concerned about here is that individual differences exist and that, except under extremely rare conditions, there is always a gap between one's potential and present level of productivity.

In the following diagram, Art has been arbitrarily given a potential (shown by the dark liquid noted by brackets) above Jane's and Fred's. Fred, on the other hand, has been given a potential below Jane's and Art's.

Now, to complete our diagram, let us assign a current productivity level to each of the three workers.

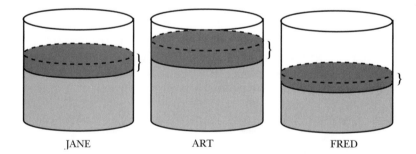

JANE                    ART                    FRED

You will note that even though Art has a higher potential than Jane, there is not a substantial difference between their current levels of performance (shown by the lighter liquid). This is a compliment to Jane, and perhaps indicates that she is more highly motivated to succeed and consequently performs closer to her potential.

Fred also deserves a compliment because the gap between his current level of productivity and his potential is smaller than that of either Jane or

Art. Fred is doing an excellent job in living up to his potential. Perhaps with more education and training, Fred will be able to raise his potential gradually and, in turn, increase his productivity.

## Group Productivity Potentials

Just as each individual has a current and potential level of productivity, so does each branch, division, or department of an organization. This we call *group productivity.*

The next diagram illustrates this important concept. The beaker represents the productivity level and potential of the department as a whole.

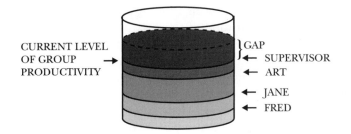

You will observe that the productivity levels of Fred, Jane, and Art have been added to that of the supervisor. As you can see, the supervisor does not contribute as much in productivity (actually getting the work out) as do the individual employees. Why not?

The answer is simple. The primary responsibility of the supervisor is to help each worker achieve his or her maximum productivity. The supervisor's secondary responsibility (as a working supervisor) is to do a certain amount of work personally. The supervisor cannot be expected to take care of the many supervisory responsibilities and also do as much work as each one of the employees in the department. The supervisor's concern is the *total department productivity,* for this is how the supervisor is measured by management.

You will also notice that there is a gap in the department beaker, just as there was in the others. This is a *departmental gap.* Just as an individual has a certain potential for productivity, so does a department.

A crew working for a telephone company might have the potential for installing 120 telephones in a certain period of time and yet actually install only 80. A retail store might have the potential for selling $5,000 worth of merchandise on a day when everything is ideal, and yet on most days sells only $2,000 worth. A claims department for an insurance company might have the potential for processing fifty claims per day, and yet may never reach this goal. Just as there is a gap with individuals, there is one with departments and organizations.

## Closing Productivity Potential Gaps

It is the responsibility of the supervisor to close the gap between what the department is currently doing and what it might do in the future. There are two ways a supervisor can help to close the gap. One is by working harder, putting in more hours and making better use of personal time. Because the supervisor is only one person, there is a limit to what he (or she) can do alone to reduce the size of the gap.

The second—and by far the more effective way to reduce the gap—is to reduce the gaps between the levels of each employee. The productivity of the department is the sum total of the productivity of all members of the department, including the supervisor. The supervisor is interested in each worker's productivity because of what each can contribute to the total.

What should this basic principle mean to you?

Simply this: All employees in a department are interdependent as far as departmental productivity is concerned. If you raise your personal productivity, but at the same time take away some of the productivity of others in the department (because of poor human relations), you have not necessarily added to the total.

Sound strange?

To demonstrate this vital fundamental, let us take Art as an example. The following diagram tells us that Art has a high potential and a good level of productivity. In fact, he is currently producing more than either Jane or Fred.

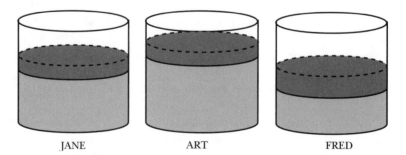

JANE                ART                FRED

But let us assume for a moment that Art begins to ignore Jane and Fred. He is no longer interested in helping them. He refuses to pitch in and do some of their work when they are absent. He starts to rub them the wrong way. His superior attitude causes resentment. Instead of natural, healthy competition, the situation becomes personal and vindictive.

What could happen then?

The productivity of Jane and Fred could drop because of the lack of harmony in the department.

Now let us see what might happen if Art does just the opposite. Let us assume that he becomes more sensitive about human relations. Instead of antagonizing Jane and Fred, he starts working with them. He takes up some of the slack when they are absent. He compliments them on certain skills. He earns their respect instead of their animosity. What happens? Harmony replaces disharmony.

Instead of a wider gap between current and potential productivity levels of Jane and Fred, there is a smaller gap as shown in the following diagram. Both Jane and Fred produce more because Art has strengthened his horizontal relationships with them.

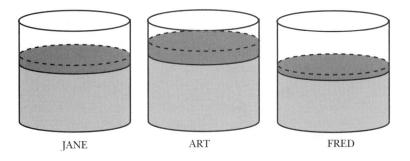

JANE        ART        FRED

This interdependence between workers in a department cannot be ignored. *Group* productivity is the key more than *individual* performance. More will be said on this when we study *Success as a Team Player* in Chapter 10.

It should be pointed out, however, that sometimes a single individual can raise her (or his) productivity above that of co-workers; and even though relationships are not ideal, the co-workers will strive to increase their personal productivity so that the other worker will not show them up. The reaction of employees in each situation is different.

Let's review what we have discussed in this chapter.

1. There is always a gap between an individual's current level of productivity and his (or her) potential. If the employee consistently has a small gap, he is trying hard to contribute and should be complimented by the supervisor for working so close to his true potential.

2. A departmental gap represents the difference between what a department can do and what it is actually doing. If the departmental gap is

small, the supervisor is doing a good job and should be complimented by her (or his) superiors.

3. The human-relations behavior of one worker affects the productivity gap of co-workers as well as that of the department.

> *Is your attitude a value-added component for your work group?*

# Case 6

**"Now you tell me . . ."**

# Message

Jeff, a hard-working specialty upholsterer, was one of several employees in a small manufacturing unit where productivity depended upon the close co-operation of everyone. Jeff had high potential and lived up to it, producing more than anyone in the unit. But Jeff liked to work alone, and he seldom volunteered to help his fellow workers. Many of the people who worked with him felt he had a superior attitude, and they resented it.

Jeff's supervisor gave a lot of thought to the problem. Although Jeff was producing at the highest level in the unit, the total productivity of the unit had actually gone down slightly since Jeff joined the group. Could it be that Jeff had done more damage (through poor human relations) than good (by his high personal productivity)? The supervisor came to the conclusion that Jeff was an outstanding employee when viewed alone, but a very poor one when viewed as a member of a group.

When Jeff's supervisor was promoted to a more responsible position, management selected someone from outside the unit to become the new supervisor. Jeff felt he should have been the one to be promoted and immediately demanded an explanation. He was told that he was the highest producer in the unit, but his human-relations skills were not up to standard. Management felt that the other workers in the unit would not respect him as their supervisor.

Do you agree with management's decision to pass over Jeff, even though Jeff was the best producer? Give reasons why you agree or disagree. How responsible do you feel the supervisor was for Jeff's being passed over? (For a suggested answer, see page 227.)

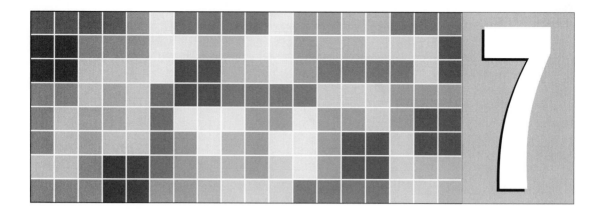

# The Winning Combination

**"High productivity and good relationships, too?"**

Thought for the Day: A happy heart, resourceful mind, and helping hands are a good combination of skills for a successful life.

There is a danger of misinterpretation in discussing human relations and productivity. You might have deduced from the last few chapters that building strong, healthy vertical and horizontal working relationships automatically results in greater departmental productivity. This is not necessarily so.

An employee can be happy, satisfied, and content with his (or her) job and yet not carry his fair share of the workload. A group of employees in a department can get along beautifully with each other, and yet the productivity of the department might be far below average.

## Happy Employees Are Usually High Producers

The goal of good human relations is not just happy employees, but *happy employees who produce more.* The goal is greater productivity and ultimately greater profit. It is theoretically possible that a business organization could devote so much time and money to making employees happy and comfortable that the company could go broke and out of business. Management is therefore not interested in making people happy just because happy people are nice to have around or because happy people stick with their jobs longer. Management is interested in making their employees happy because happy employees, under the right leadership, can be motivated to achieve greater productivity.

Management's focus on productivity should not be interpreted as meaning employers are sensitive to their employees' needs only because they are interested in increasing productivity. Not true. Nevertheless, management (and their employees) must fully accept the economic truth that survival under free competition requires a continual improvement in personal and group productivity.

Employees who are fun to be around but never get down to doing their share of the work are a burden on fellow workers. They are parasites on the productivity of others. They may be pleasant to have around, but they are far too expensive for management to keep. Why?

- The work itself must be done.

- Labor costs must be controlled.

- Customers must be well served.

Greater productivity must be the goal of American business organizations if they are to survive and compete with other world markets where labor costs are much lower. The development and use of more and more highly technical equipment will take us a long way, but human productivity must do the rest.

It is only natural, then, that management should seek outstanding people for jobs that are increasingly sophisticated. It is only natural that they should try to find, hire, and train people who have already developed their human-relations skills to a high level.

## Essential Work Skills

What are the human factors management seeks?

The most important one is the *right combination of personal productivity and human relations.* The best way to explain this fundamental is to present the situation of a small department composed of three employees who have identical assignments and similar workloads. For example, Alice and Richard have been employed in their positions for over a year. Hazel, on the other hand, recently joined the organization as a replacement for an employee who resigned. She has a very high potential, substantially above that of the other two people.

Alice and Richard have been taking it very easy, and there is a sizable gap between their current level of productivity and their potential. In other words, they have not been motivated to do the kind of job they can do. Hazel, however, is very ambitious. She wants to build a reputation for herself and, if possible, move on quickly to a supervisory position where she will have more responsibility and remuneration. In order to gain the attention of management, Hazel decides to increase her personal level of productivity to the point where it will surpass both Alice's and Richard's. She has decided she can further her career in either of two ways:

1. Hazel can go all out and pass Alice and Richard in a hurry. But in using this approach, she would risk building poor horizontal working relationships with her fellow workers.

2. Hazel can pass Alice and Richard in personal productivity on a somewhat slower and less obvious schedule. That is, she can concentrate on building good horizontal relationships with her fellow workers and create a harmonious environment that will increase their productivity along with her own.

What might happen if Hazel decided to follow the first approach and ignore building good horizontal relationships?

It is possible, of course, that Alice and Richard might become motivated. Perhaps in order to make their positions more secure, they might compete with Hazel, and as a result the productivity of the entire department might increase.

On the other hand, it is just as likely that the outcome will not be positive. Alice and Richard might resent Hazel and, rather than work with her, might in subtle ways work against her. For example, because they are more experienced, they might let her make some mistakes that, if they wanted to, they could prevent. They could do many little things that would make her uncomfortable and her work more difficult. As a result, Hazel might become critical of Alice and Richard, and the relationships among the three could deteriorate to the point where the productivity of all three would drop. A drop in group productivity would be especially serious if customers were involved.

Lowered productivity for the group might not happen, of course—but it could. And if it did, Hazel would certainly not have helped her future with the company. It is not a safe approach for her to take. She could be asking for trouble.

Now what might happen if Hazel took the opposite approach—if she passed Alice and Richard in personal productivity, but at the same time worked hard to build good, strong working relationships with them?

It is likely that Hazel would make her job easier. She would be valued more by the supervisor. She would earn the support of both Alice and Richard. She would contribute more to productivity. Instead of falling into a human-relations trap, she would demonstrate to management that she had insight and sensitivity.

Of course, it would be easy to tell Hazel that building good working relationships with Alice and Richard is the best route to take. But how should she go about doing it? Here are four suggestions:

1. Hazel could build better horizontal relationships with Alice and Richard by sacrificing a little of her personal productivity to help increase theirs. She could accomplish her objectivity of building better relationships by looking for opportunities to help Alice and Richard when their workloads are heavy or when they do not feel well. She could also pitch in when one of them is absent.

2. As Hazel brings her personal productivity above that of Alice and Richard, she should be careful not to become critical of them because their performance levels are now lower than hers. She should not expect constant praise from her supervisor just because she, at this point in her career, is carrying a larger share of the work load.

3. Hazel should be careful not to isolate herself too much from Alice and Richard. Even if she is occasionally rejected by them, she must continue to be pleasant until good relationships are built. She must be sincerely interested in both Alice and Richard as individuals in order to win their respect. A superior attitude on her part will defeat any effort she makes to build sound relationships.

4. Above all, Hazel should stand on her own two feet and work out her own problems without complaining or running to the supervisor for help. She can achieve the support of Alice and Richard only by demonstrating to them that she knows what she is doing and can fight her own battles.

Hazel will go a long way in communicating to management that she has one of the human-relations plus factors they seek if she keeps the following principle in mind: An increase in personal productivity should be accompanied by increased attention to horizontal relationships.

So what strategy did Hazel use?

Last week Hazel was invited to have a long talk with the human resource director of her company. During the conversation she asked the director what kind of a person management was really seeking. The director said that management usually sought four plus factors in the employees they hoped to promote into management. Hazel made a big effort to remember all four, and this is the way she would probably put it if you asked her about them now.

## The Person Management Is Looking for Is

1. *. . . someone who strives to work close to her (or his) personal potential regardless of the level at which fellow workers are performing.* She is always trying to close her personal productivity gap, even if others are content to do only what they have to in order to keep their jobs. She is self-motivating. She takes a professional approach to her job and gains real satisfaction when she does it well.

2. *. . . someone who is never completely satisfied with her personal potential.* She believes that she can always improve it a little. She truly believes in lifelong learning. She takes advantage of any training that the company will provide. She continues to read and study on her own. She is always learning more and more about the job ahead of her. She may even continue her formal education by attending classes at a nearby adult education center, junior college, or university. Although she is realistic about her potential, she does not go along with the idea that a person is born with a certain potential that cannot be changed. She will continue to learn and to prepare for new opportunities.

3. *. . . someone who believes human relations is important.* She puts people and the development of good human-relations skills ahead of machines, statistics, procedures, and credentials. She accepts responsibility for building strong relationships as an interesting and inevitable challenge. She is highly productive, and at the same time she protects her relationships with people. She does this with a sense of humor and personal understanding. She is proud of the fact that she is a good person with whom most people like to work. She endeavors to keep all relations on a sincere level. She does all of this because she knows that she contributes to the productivity of her department in two ways: through her personal work effort and through the relationships she builds with her fellow employees. She refuses to sacrifice one for the other, and she constantly tries to keep them in proper balance.

4. . . . *someone who makes a point of being loyal to her company or organiza-*
*tion.* Being loyal does not mean that she automatically accepts all of the
policies and practices that filter down from the top. Far from it. She ac-
cepts the responsibility for making changes, but she remains loyal to her
company while fighting for changes. She feels that her company deserves
her best effort. She refuses to let human-relations problems, the negative
attitudes of others, or personal disappointments slow her down.

Hazel asked the director a second question: "How many employees will
I find in this company who have all of the four plus factors?"

He replied: "It is impossible to say. There are many who are good at one or
two, some who are good at three, but only a few who are good at all four. At any
rate, those who demonstrate all four do not remain line employees for long, unless by choice, because they are desperately needed for supervisory positions."

Hazel then posed her last question: "How does management single out
those who have the plus factors they seek?"

"It's easy," replied the director. "You only have to be slightly taller than
others to stand out in the crowd. It's the same with the plus factors. You
don't have to be miles ahead of others for management to recognize you; a
little is all it takes."

## Productivity Ultimately Involves the Quality of Service Provided to Customers

When new employees enter the work force, their main interest is usually career advancement. Advancement is encouraged because a strong focus on personal goals is motivating and has many other beneficial aspects to both
employee and employer. But if self-interest goes too far, it can detract from the
responsibility to fulfill job duties. A primary responsibility, often neglected
by otherwise excellent employees, is developing an effective *service attitude.*

A service attitude is a desire to satisfy customers to the point where
they will continue to use the firm's services and bring in new clients as
well. All employees should take time to identify who their customers are
and then serve them in every way possible with a positive attitude. Imple-
menting a customer service strategy will create a win-win situation for the
client and the company. The result? *Career advancement will be facilitated*
*for the employee.*

It is easy to identify clients when you are on the front line providing
direct customer service. A waitress, bank teller, doctor, or salesperson receives daily reminders. But what about a machinist, software engineer, or
hospital dietitian? Although these individuals may not service clients directly, they all have service-attitude responsibilities.

The machinist's client may be a manufacturer who assembles parts he (or
she) builds into kitchen appliances. Thus, the service attitude of the machinist

involves building durable parts, meeting production schedules, and conforming to specifications. The machinist may never see the client, but he is building a quality product that serves the client indirectly. The hospital dietitian serves those who will eat the food prepared by others. The software engineer's clients are those who will eventually utilize the computer programs. All can benefit from a positive *service attitude.*

To illustrate how productivity and customer service must be linked, here's a good example.

> **Sid and Lisette.** Both Sid and Lisette design computer software for financial institutions. Both are highly professional and career minded. The primary difference between them is their service attitudes.
>
> Sid works closely with his own boss and the manager of the financial organization being served to get the specifics of each job before designing his software package. He does not take time to consult with the ultimate users—tellers and other front-line employees. Even so, Sid receives many compliments from his boss because he is always on or ahead of schedule.
>
> Lisette, on the other hand, takes the time to get specifics directly from users (branch managers, new account officers, tellers), who are the ultimate clients. This takes more time, so Lisette does not always receive immediate reinforcement from her boss. Most of the time her compliments show up later, but they are more meaningful because they demonstrate a superior service attitude.
>
> Each individual must identify her (or his) clients and design a strategy that will best serve them, whether compliments are received or not.

Your job success will depend, to a large degree, on finding a proper balance of personal productivity and human relations that works for you. It should not be difficult to determine how you can help your co-workers if you are seriously concerned about building good working relationships. Learning about their needs as well as those of your customers will also help you to learn more about yourself and how you can improve your own productivity and work quality.

## Total Quality

In recent years, most employees have been exposed to the Total Quality movement. Employers, in an effort to keep customers happy, have focused on getting workers to find ways of reducing inefficiencies while providing value-added elements to products and services. The Total Quality model has become vitally important to most organizations where change, especially in the way people think and interact, promotes a good balance between productivity and human relations. Familiar terms starting with Total Quality Management (TQM) and more recently Continuous Quality Improvement (CQI) and Total Quality have evolved from emphasis being placed on quality control, process improvement, customer service, and operations improvement.

The Total Quality movement has come a long way since Total Quality Management (TQM) became a popular management philosophy in the early

1990s. TQM and its many quality-related offshoots have helped organizations change toward becoming more competitive and profitable. As an all-encompassing process that involves the attitudes of everyone in an organization, the basics of TQM is to improve every aspect of customer service and product quality. It involves the following:

- **Accountability.** A basic concept in TQM is that everyone is responsible for improving their performance which is to be measured over and over again based upon facts. TQM embraces the idea that "what gets measured gets improved."

- **Focus on Customer.** Under TQM everything starts with the customer and filters back to the production process. To achieve quality means to exceed customer expectations.

- **Group Decisions.** Whenever all members of the team are involved in the decision-making process everyone assumes more responsibility to make it work. To make TQM work, an organization must rely on the entire work force.

- **Commitment to Improvement.** The Total Quality commitment never ends. It is a continuous movement. A successful TQM firm is devoted to improve product and service long before the customer becomes dissatisfied or competition gains an advantage.

As you may have already guessed, the Total Quality movement is an *attitude* of management to promote a learning organization by generating action plans to improve product and service at every turn.

## A Winning Equation

To summarize the importance of a proper balance of personal productivity and human relations, consider a somewhat "theatrical" redefinition of Einstein's theory for mass energy equivalence, $E = mc^2$. That is, a "winning equation" is created by redefining the terms of the equation as follows:

E = energy and enthusiasm to work hard,

m = motivation to build strong relationships, and

c = commitment to continuously strive for self-improvement.

> *Every day of your life, put into practice the winning equation,*
> $E = mc^2$.*

---

*See definition of $E = mc^2$ as noted in text above.

# Case 7

**"Okay, next time I'll cool it."**

# Insight

Ted, an air conditioning journeyman, had been with a large appliance repair company for more than nine months. From his first day, he had been determined to set a pace that would earn him a promotion. It took Ted a little while to catch on to the job, but within four months he was up to the average of others in productivity. After a few more months, he was the top producer in the department. In the meantime, his co-workers maintained a steady but slower pace.

Ted felt good about his ability to pass others in the department, but he was disturbed because he had received so little recognition for his achievement. In fact, the harder he worked, the more difficult it was to get along with the others. Even his supervisor had failed to give Ted as much encouragement as he felt he deserved.

After a few weeks as top producer, Ted became more critical of his co-workers. He started to give out a few tips on how they might improve their efficiency, and he began to sound off more in staff meetings.

One day the whole situation reached a boiling point. Ted was called into the supervisor's office and was strongly counseled to be more patient and understanding with his fellow workers. "Look, Ted," said his supervisor. "you have everything going for you, but you will never win a promotion if you blow your cool with your fellow employees. You have very high potential and your productivity is great, but you can't expect others to always equal your pace. I don't want you to destroy now the very relationships you might have to rebuild later should you take my place."

Was Ted's exasperation justified? Or did his supervisor have a good point? (For a suggested answer, see page 227.)

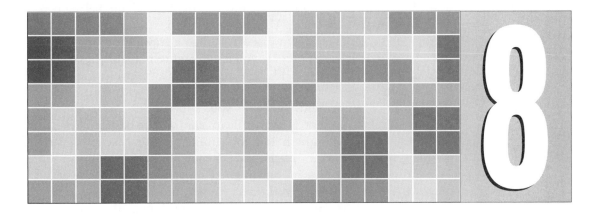

# Your Most Important Working Relationship

**"I understand my supervisor perfectly."**

Thought for the Day: The quality of any relationship is dependent upon the quality of communications.

The most important working relationship you have is the one between you and your immediate supervisor. This single relationship can speed up your personal progress or slow it down to a discouraging crawl. It can make going to work a joy or a drag. It can prepare you for greater responsibilities or it can frustrate your desire to learn. And there is just no way to avoid the human-relations fact that, good or bad, you must learn to cope with your boss.

What kind of person will you get as your supervisor?

It is impossible to predict. However, he (or she) will be basically the same person he used to be when he held a job similar to yours, except that now he has much more responsibility. He may or may not have been given some special training to help him become a good supervisor. He may be easy to get along with or he may be very difficult. He may be sensitive to your needs or he may be insensitive. He may be feeling his way along and making many mistakes, or he may be highly experienced and a real pro at his job.

Three things are certain about your supervisor:

1. She (or he) probably has a strong personality that gave her the confidence to become a supervisor in the first place.

2. The responsibilities of being a supervisor probably weigh heavily on her shoulders.

3. She has work authority over you.

## The Supervisor's Role

What is a supervisor?

- **Teacher**   He (or she) is a *teacher*. He will not only teach you the routine of your new job, but he will also have a great influence on your attitude toward your job and the company. He has a reservoir of knowledge, skills, and techniques that you need to learn. You will be most fortunate if he is a good teacher. If he is not, you will have to learn from observation.

- **Counselor**   He is a *counselor*. His job is to see that you live up to your potential. He may need to correct errors you are making. He may need to give you tips on improving yourself as an employee. He may feel the need to have a heart-to-heart talk with you at times.

- **Leader**   He is a *leader*. More than anything else, your supervisor must provide the leadership your department requires. He must provide motivation for all employees. He must earn your respect—not by being soft and easy, but by being a strong leader who will help you build a long-range career.

It would be a mistake to attempt to type supervisors. They cannot be clearly classified into different groups. Each supervisor has a unique personality. Each has her (or his) own style.

Do you recall your early school days, when you discovered the differences between teachers? You may have had one who expected much more from you than the others. You may not have liked that person at the time, but years later you came to realize how much that one teacher had taught you. The same can be true with supervisors.

If you are ambitious, you don't want an easygoing supervisor who does not care and, as a result, hinders instead of helps your progress. You will be better off with a more concerned, more demanding supervisor who will help you reach your potential. With an easy supervisor, you might develop some poor working habits and eventually become unhappy with yourself. With a strong supervisor—one who will take time to train you—you will become a better worker and improve your future. But no matter what kind of boss you encounter, it is up to you to learn to understand him (or her) and work efficiently under his kind of leadership.

*You* should do some of the adjusting.

*You* should provide some of the understanding.

*You* should help build the relationship that must exist between the two of you.

## Working Climates

Each individual supervisor creates her (or his) own special climate, or atmosphere, under which you must operate. The following analysis of three kinds of climates may give you some indication of the adjustments you might have to make in the future.

1. **The Structured Climate.** Some supervisors are more strict than others. They operate a tight department by keeping close, and sometimes restrictive, controls. They frequently expect employees to be precisely on time, orderly, and highly efficient. They permit foolishness only when a special occasion calls for it. Ninety-eight percent of the time they stick strictly to business.

   The supervisor who creates this kind of atmosphere often appears cold, distant, and unfeeling to the new employee. He (or she) seems unreachable. As a result, the new employee may begin to fear this person.

   Some jobs force supervisors to be autocratic. Some kinds of work require very high safety standards and efficiency. For example, a producer of a television program might have to be autocratic in order to maintain the split-second efficiency required. Work of a highly technical nature, in which certain precision standards must be met, will call for a different climate than work in a service field.

   Although the supervisor who establishes a structured atmosphere may appear cold and unapproachable, the opposite is often true. The supervisor is probably more interested in you and more willing to help than you suspect.

2. **The Permissive Climate.** The direct opposite of the structured climate is the permissive atmosphere. Some supervisors have a free-and-easy leadership style. There is no apparent intervention, and there are few controls or restrictions.

   The permissive climate can be the most dangerous of all, especially for the inexperienced employee because his (or her) need for self-discipline is so great. The employee who does not feel the presence of a leader may not make good use of time. The employee may find it difficult to develop self-motivation. If things are too easygoing, the employee may relax too much and become too friendly with fellow workers. All of this can create bad habits that will ultimately lead to mutual dissatisfaction. Instead of being an ideal situation, then, the permissive climate becomes a trap that can destroy the desire to succeed and eventually cause great unhappiness.

   Whether we like to accept it or not, a structured climate often gives us more job security and forces us to live closer to our potential. Beware of a climate that is too relaxed unless you are a self-starter and can discipline yourself. You might discover that too much freedom is your downfall.

3. **The Democratic Climate.** The goal of most supervisors in modern organizations is to create a democratic climate. A democratic atmosphere is the most difficult of all to establish. In fact, purely democratic action is often a goal rather than a reality.

   A democratic climate is one in which employees want to do what the supervisor wants done. The supervisor becomes one of the group and still retains her (or his) leadership role. The employees are permitted to have a lot to say about the operation of the department. Everyone becomes involved because each person works from inside the group rather than from outside. The supervisor is the leader and a member of the group at the same time. As a result, a team feeling is created. Many isolated cases of research indicate that most people experience greater personal satisfaction and respond with greater productivity if the supervisor can create and maintain a democratic atmosphere.

   Then why can't more supervisors achieve a democratic climate? There are many reasons.

   In the first place, the democratic climate is the most difficult climate to create, and once created, the most difficult to maintain. It requires a real expert, an individual with great skill and sensitivity; *one should not expect to find a large number of supervisors with this ability.*

   In the second place, not all workers respond to a democratic climate, ideal as it may seem. You may like it best, but others in your department may like a more autocratic approach. This is especially true when there are young workers in a department where many more experienced and older employees work. You will often hear employees say: "I wish he would quit fooling around and tell us what to do" or "I wish she would tighten up things around here—people are getting away with murder" or "He is too easy. I can't enjoy working for someone who doesn't set things down clearly and specifically from the beginning."

In the third place, the supervisor who aspires to build a true democratic climate always exists somewhere between the structured and the permissive. The supervisor may approach the ideal situation for a while, only to find that a few employees are taking advantage of the situation. When this happens it is necessary to tighten up again and become more structured.

All supervisors must create and maintain what some people refer to as a *discipline line.* A discipline line is an imaginary line or point beyond which the employee senses she (or he) should not pass lest some form of disapproval and possible disciplinary action take place. It is important to keep a consistent discipline line. Some supervisors claim that keeping a firm but comfortable line is a tightrope they walk each day on the job.

## Supervisory Styles

You may hear your supervisor or a college professor discuss Theory X and Theory Y, what Douglas McGregor identified as assumptions that mold behavior. What are they?

- **Theory X**   (representing a more structured climate) supports management by control. It states that the worker should be directed and controlled in order to achieve high productivity. A basic assumption is that most employees are not self-motivated. Leaders with a Theory X orientation often reach consistently high productivity levels in their departments. They also have the reputation of doing an excellent job in training their employees.

- **Theory Y**   (representing a more democratic/permissive climate) encourages participative management. It states that workers will achieve greater productivity if they can set their own goals and direct their own efforts through involvement. The theory assumes that under the proper working climate, workers will motivate themselves. A discipline line is maintained at a lower level. Theory Y leaders who are sufficiently skillful to achieve high productivity demonstrate a high level of leadership talent that often attracts the attention of upper management.

Every supervisor creates an individual climate. Some supervisors come up with a workable blend of the structured and democratic. Others come up with a blend of the permissive and democratic. We call this blend their *management,* or *leadership, style.*

Whether we personally like a supervisor or like his (or her) style is not as important as whether we can learn to be productive in the climate the person creates. A new worker should not be too quick to judge, however, because it is often true that what appears to be a difficult climate at the beginning might turn out to be a comfortable and beneficial one later on. So whatever *style* your supervisor has, it will be your responsibility to build the best possible relationship with him (or her). Your career progress may depend upon it. To help you meet this challenge, here are ten tips that should assist you.

1. *Avoid transferring to your supervisor the negative attitudes you may have developed toward other authority figures in your life.* Some people who have had problems with other supervisors, parents, teachers, and similar authority figures make the mistake of transferring their feelings of hostility to their new supervisor. This is unfair. Wipe away any previous negative feelings you may have and give your new (or present) boss an opportunity for her (or him) to build a healthy relationship with you. If you give her a fair chance, she will almost always earn your respect instead of your hostility.

2. *Expect some rough days under your boss's supervision.* Everyone, including a supervisor, is entitled to a few bad days. Your boss is only human. If she should boil over on a given day, don't let it throw you. If she seems to be picking on you for a while, give her time to get over it. More important than anything else, try not to take personally anything she does that you don't like. There may be times when you do not understand your boss's behavior, but if you can float along with it, chances are good that it won't last long.

3. *Refuse to nurse a small gripe into a major issue.* A small gripe, when nurtured, can get blown out of proportion and can lead to a confrontation with your supervisor that will hurt your relationship. If you have a legitimate gripe, try to talk it over with her quickly so you can get it out of your system before it builds up. Remember, she won't know you have a complaint unless you tell her.

4. *Select the right time to approach your supervisor.* Whether you have a complaint or a positive suggestion to make, try to approach your supervisor at the right time. She may be too busy or under too much pressure on a given day to talk to you. If so, wait it out. When the pressure is off, chances are good she will give you a fair opportunity. However, if you do try to talk to her at a bad time and are turned off, wait until another day and try again. If it is important to you, she will no doubt want to talk to you about it. Give her another chance.

5. *Never go over your supervisor's head without talking to her first.* The easiest and quickest way to destroy your relationship with your supervisor is to go over her head on a problem that involves her unit or department. Always talk to your supervisor first. If you are not satisfied with the results,

you can then take other action. At least this way your supervisor will know that you consulted her first.

6. *Try not to let your supervisor intimidate you.* Keep in mind that she may not be a professional. She could be guilty of playing favorites and other forms of nonprofessional behavior. Such behavior could cause you to fear your boss. Fear is a strong emotion. If you become so fearful of your boss that you cannot approach her, you should talk to someone in the human resources department, consider a possible transfer, or if necessary, resign. You will never be happy working for a person you fear, and a supervisor will seldom respect you if you are afraid of her.

7. *It can be a human-relations mistake to make a buddy of your supervisor.* Your relationship with your supervisor is a business relationship. Keep it that way. The distance between you and your boss may often appear to be a fine line, but she is still your boss. If you get too personal, it will almost always turn out badly.

8. *In case you make a mistake, clear the air quickly.* If you make a serious goof and injure your relationship with your boss, why not clean the slate with an open discussion? It is a good idea to leave work every day with a pleasant feeling toward your job and your supervisor. If you have had trouble with her on a given day and truly believe that it is partly your fault, the mature thing to do is to accept your share of the blame. You will feel better and so will your supervisor.

9. *Not all supervisors enjoy their roles.* A surprising number of supervisors would really prefer to be workers, but they have accepted their promotions because management has pressed them to do so, because they feel they can contribute more as supervisors, or because they can make more money to help their families. As an employee, you should view this as a possibility. It will give you more insight into the role itself and perhaps help you tolerate your supervisor more easily. Try to remember that being a good supervisor is difficult. Sometimes those who try the hardest to win the respect of their workers never fully succeed because of personality traits they cannot change.

10. *When possible, convert your supervisor into a mentor.* A mentor is a person in a key position who takes a personal interest in your career and acts as an adviser. Your present supervisor may be on her way up in your organization. If you build the right relationship with her, she might counsel and guide you over a period of time, even though she may no longer be your supervisor. You might even ride her coattails to the top.

It should be remembered, however, that ethical behavior on the part of both you and your supervisor is essential if the relationship is to be strong and lasting. To maintain your side of the bargain, the following tips are presented.

- Maintain open and honest communication. Tell the whole story regarding any problems that develop. The moment deception appears, the relationship is permanently injured.

- Do not discuss your supervisor in a negative way with co-workers. It communicates an absence of loyalty and is considered by many to be unethical. You need not approve of everything your supervisor does, but it is best to keep your attitude to yourself.

- Refuse to be influenced by either your supervisor or co-workers to perform unethical acts. A good way to take your stand on any questionable situation is to ask openly: "Is this ethical?"

In summary, building and maintaining a strong, warm, productive relationship with your boss is a real human-relations challenge. It isn't always easy. Yet, it is an essential step in your progress. You may be used to one supervisor, only to discover that you have been transferred to another department and have to start from scratch. Every relationship will be a unique challenge. Make the most of every experience.

> *Positive relationships are built from positive behaviors transmitted by a positive attitude.*

# Case 8

**"I'm a Theory Y person myself."**

# Choice

Carol is a customer service representative with an e-commerce organization. For the last sixty days she has been training for a new position and assignment. She has just received word to report to the human resource department to discuss her new role in the company.

The director gives her a choice of assignments. She tells Carol that two departments have requested her services. The departments are identical in their operations. The only difference is the type of climate created by each supervisor.

One department has a rather demanding supervisor who has a leadership style that leans in the direction of Theory X. He is an old-timer and has been in charge of his department for many years. He expects and gets high productivity and loyalty from all his employees. Everyone admits that he has trained more people who are now in top management positions than anyone in the company.

The other department is run by an up-and-coming younger supervisor who adheres to Theory Y. She tries to get everyone in the department to participate in decisions and get involved. She prides herself on her democratic leadership style and feels she has been very successful. People appear to be very happy working for her. The personnel turnover is lower in this department than in the other. Productivity is slightly higher.

Which department would you select? On what basis? (For a suggested answer, see page 228.)

# Understanding the Nature of Relationships

**"People are easy to figure."**

Thought for the Day: Don't confuse your assumptions (biased or not) with facts—ingrained assumptions have wrecked many potentially good relationships.

As we delve more deeply into the nature of working relationships, there are several characteristics that have a considerable influence on the quality or tone of the relationship. In a sense, they constitute the ingredients, or components, of the relationship itself. In this chapter we will look into six major characteristics that represent human-relations competencies you may wish to possess as you consider the nature of past, present, and future working relationships.

The idea of a relationship may be easier to understand if you visualize it as an invisible tunnel between two fellow employees. Disregard the personalities involved and concentrate on the relationship itself. The following illustrations may help you do this.

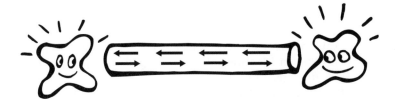

The two-way arrows between the amoebas remind us that verbal communication is the lifeblood of the relationship. Good input and good reception are necessary at both ends. The following illustration adds to the relationship the six factors we will discuss in this chapter.

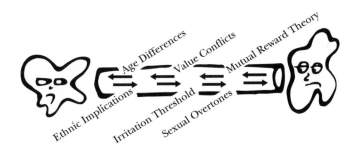

Of course, not all of the elements in this illustration are likely to be present in any single relationship. Some relationships may have only one or two. Others may have four or five. An investigation into each of them, however, will give you additional insight into the nature of all working relationships.

# Mutual Reward Theory

With proper care, you can create working relationships that will turn out to be mutually rewarding. The *mutual reward theory (MRT)* states that a relationship between two people is enhanced when there is a satisfactory balance of rewards between them. In a good MRT relationship, both parties come out ahead. In fact, if a working relationship is to remain healthy over a long time, it must contribute something of value to both persons. When one individual suddenly discovers that she (or he) has been contributing substantially more than she has been receiving, the relationship can quickly weaken. However, when there is a balanced reward system between people, the working relationship can thrive. The cases of Gina and Molly illustrate this theory.

> **Gina.**   Gina was a quiet, timid, serious worker with outstanding job knowledge. A co-worker, Joe, on the other hand, was a very outgoing person with great personal confidence but less job knowledge. They worked next to each other in identical jobs and, despite their differences, they slowly built a strong relationship.
>
> How did it happen? Gina made a patient effort to teach Joe as much as possible about the job and took care of some mistakes he made without the supervisor's finding out about them. What did Joe do in return? He helped Gina develop more self-confidence and become a more outgoing person. He paid her well-deserved compliments, introduced her to co-workers from other departments, and generally gave her a feeling of acceptance that she had not been able to develop by herself. Because each party contributed to the success of the other (both eventually became supervisors), their relationship became strong and permanent.
>
> **Molly.**   Molly worked for Ms. Gonzales for three years before taking over her job as department manager. During that period, MRT was constantly in effect. Molly provided high productivity, loyalty, and dependability to the department and to Ms. Gonzales. Ms. Gonzales, as the supervisor, provided a good learning environment for Molly and gave her the recognition she needed. For example, Ms. Gonzales often introduced Molly to upper-management people and related the progress she was making. This exposure eventually gave Molly the edge she needed to achieve a promotion.

The term *bonding* is frequently used to signify a close, emotionally important relationship. Bonding can take place between two co-workers, between an employee and an immediate supervisor, and especially between an employee and a mentor. A working relationship that involves bonding needs to have two characteristics. First, it is important that the relationship not become overly personal to the point where the present productivity and future career of either individual are placed in jeopardy. Second, it is vital to the longevity of the relationship that it be mutually rewarding so both parties benefit somewhat equally.

Relationships can almost always be mutually rewarding because people can strengthen each other in many different ways. Obviously, however, when one person does all the giving, deterioration sets in quickly. As you build new relationships and protect old ones, look for things you can do to contribute to the success and happiness of the person next to you. When you help others, you will almost always receive something in return that will make life better for you. If you weave MRT into your behavior, you demonstrate a significant human-relations competency.

# Value Conflicts

Everyone has his (or her) own value system. And everyone has his own priority list of what is really important in life. Different people seek different lifestyles. It is only natural that value conflicts exist between people who are forced to associate with each other closely in the world of work. Here are two typical examples.

**Tony.** Tony was assigned to work next to Mr. Henderson who was more than twice his age. Tony was single, energetic, and enjoyed a rather flamboyant social life. It was no secret that Tony did not want to assume family responsibilities too soon and he was determined to have a lifestyle different from that of his parents. Tony's foreign sports car and fashionable clothing reflected this attitude. Mr. Henderson, on the other hand, was a family oriented, religious person.

How did they learn to work together gracefully? At the beginning, they both played it cool and built their relationship exclusively on the basis of job factors. Tony learned to respect Mr. Henderson for his many years of job experience and his willingness to share it. Mr. Henderson learned to respect Tony for his willingness to learn and contribute a full day's work. After six months they could even discuss their value differences. A better mutual understanding resulted.

**Beverly.** Beverly was brought up in a strict home environment and was taught to respect discipline. She was considered fairly square by her contemporaries. Her co-worker, Trish, on the other hand, was very happy-go-lucky and undisciplined. Trish considered herself very much ahead of others of her generation. How did Beverly and Trish get along when they were forced to work very closely together? At first, the sparks of conflict were rather obvious. But slowly they built a sound working relationship based upon their mutual desire to do a good job for the company and further their careers. They did not become close personal friends, and they did not go out together socially. However, they learned to respect each other, and both benefited from the working relationship despite their value differences.

It is a mistake, perhaps even an invasion of privacy, to impose one's own values on another, especially in the work environment. What a fellow worker does with her (or his) private life is her own business and should have nothing to do with the relationship you build with her on the job. To react to an individual in a negative way for what she does on the outside should be avoided. Common interests on the job should provide a sufficient basis for a good working relationship. You will be surprised how many good working relationships you can build with people who think and live differently than you do.

## Ethnic Implications

Only in recent years has a major attitude change come about in the United States, getting away from what some had envisioned the nation would become—one culture, with a single language and distinct traditions. Instead, today the U.S. is like a "great mosaic" created out of different cultures, and most businesses have made concerted efforts to truly address the diverse issues associated with this change.

International business, e-commerce, and the increased awareness of the critical need to promote diversity in the workplace have opened up opportunities for women and other minority groups especially in positions of authority which traditionally have been dominated by white males. More and more companies, within and outside the United States, are involved in international e-business. As a result, businesses have become much more concerned with employing and meeting the needs of the growing diverse populations that make up our culture.

In addition to more women and young people in the work force, there are also significant numbers of working Asians, Africans, and Latin Americans, especially in U.S. and multi-nationally owned and operated businesses. Depending on your organization, you can react to this demographic workplace change in three different ways:

1. If you are in the dominant culture, you can maintain a negative attitude toward others, but you may never learn to work with others successfully. In turn, your career may suffer.

2. If you are in a minority culture, you can try so hard to be one of "them" that you lose your own identity at great expense to your own positive attitude and job productivity.

3. Regardless of the position you occupy, if you adapt to all cultures in your organization you will become a better person, you will be more productive, and your career will be enhanced.

Accepting the last premise, an "international" or "mosaic" view may assist you in building strong and lasting relationships with the many different people you will meet in your workplace. It will also help you maintain your positive attitude.

A basic human-relations competency is to respect and treat every person as a unique, special individual. Look beyond outward appearances, ignore how he (or she) might resemble someone with whom you had an unfavorable experience, and accept each person as a unique individual. If everyone could sincerely adhere to this one fundamental practice, relationships would have a good chance of functioning harmoniously. Each person—and each relationship—would stand on its own, without reference to ethnic background. Unfortunately for all of us, not enough people practice this principle. Here are two short cases to illustrate the point.

**Jean.**  Jean, a middle-aged Anglo who grew up in an ethnically diverse community, had always believed she was free of prejudice, but had never worked with anyone other than co-workers from her own ethnic background. When Hobart, a young African American, joined the department, Jean realized she felt a bit uneasy and apprehensive as to how she and Hobart would get along.

Jean found Hobart to be a very easygoing, friendly person and everything started out fine with their working relationship. However, when Hobart began making mistakes and, in Jean's opinion, began asking stupid questions, Hobart definitely was not living up to her expectations. Jean became so frustrated over the matter that she was tempted to go to her supervisor.

In thinking about what she would discuss with her supervisor, Jean realized that she was expecting more of Hobart than she was of her co-workers. Without a doubt, she seemed to be looking for things to complain about Hobart's work instead of being understanding. To try to get the relationship back on a fair footing, Jean called Hobart aside and admitted her mistake. It was a good move because Hobart had felt Jean's negative attitude and wanted to build a better relationship himself.

**Arnold.**  When Arnold, a bright young Asian, went to work for a moving company, he was assigned to work with Jose on a moving van. Arnold was a community college graduate who hoped eventually to get into management. Jose was a high school graduate with over three years' experience in the moving and storage business.

Arnold learned quickly that Jose was an outstanding worker with excellent skills, but he didn't like to talk much. In fact, Jose communicated only when it was necessary to get the job done.

After two months of working as a team, Arnold could stand the silence no longer. Having made many attempts to get a light conversation going, Arnold concluded that Jose did not like him and had a lot of deep-seated hostility toward Asians. Arnold's need to converse just made him bitter about the situation. Should he ask for a transfer? Should he resign?

As Arnold thought about what he could do to get Jose to talk with him, he decided to ask Jose to join him after work at a small Latino pub near Jose's home. Arnold learned a lot about Jose that night. Jose had been pushed around by many people. He did not feel accepted. His silence was more a defense than anything else. But what got to Arnold was the fact that Jose felt that Arnold was against *him*, and not the other way around.

The discussion was a revelation for both Arnold and Jose, and much of the tension that had been present on the job was gone the next day. They had learned how to communicate and, as a result, became a better team. Arnold and Jose didn't become personal friends, but they gained a high degree of mutual respect.

There are many relationships ahead of you that will involve people from different ethnic backgrounds. These relationships will not always be easy to build and maintain. Sometimes they may demand more perception than you possess. Yet, if you are open, honest, sincere, and willing to talk, your chances of building sound MRT relationships are excellent. Keep in mind, though, that discussions of religious, political, and cultural differences do not belong in the workplace. If you judge others in ways they do not wish to be judged, they may do the same to you.

## Sexual Overtones and Harassment

Working relationships between employees frequently contain sexual overtones. For the most part, this sexual tension is not dangerous and has little important influence on productivity one way or the other. But not always. Take the case of Judy.

> **Judy.** Judy was attracted physically to her supervisor from the moment he was transferred to her department. A perceptive observer would have noticed that immediately she started wearing the best clothes in her wardrobe. She became more particular about her makeup. She started working harder to win the favor of her new boss and to create more opportunities to talk with him on business matters.
>
> The other women in Judy's department quickly sensed the sexual overtones to the relationship, and their positive attitude toward Judy began to cool. They became more distant, less willing to help her, and less tolerant of her mistakes. It didn't take long for a certain strain to develop among all the employees in the department, and productivity began to suffer.

Judy's case raises a very difficult question: *What are the human-relations dangers involved in dating someone where you work?*

There is little danger involved, provided that the individual is not your supervisor, she (or he) works in a section separated from yours, and you are smart enough to keep your business and personal worlds separate. Under these circumstances, management will probably be very understanding.

There are some real dangers, however, when working relationships have sexual overtones. Most will occur in the following ways: (1) when a supervisor dates someone in his (or her) own department, immediate cries of favoritism are raised and productivity is lost; (2) when two people—especially if they are in the same division—do not keep their business and personal worlds separate, relationships with others are hurt and eventually productivity is lowered; and (3) when one or both parties become involved or get married, a sticky situation is created that can produce harmful gossip, reduce productivity, and sometimes make it necessary for management to intervene.

Before you create or engage in a personal relationship where you work, you should also consider the chance of a later breakup between the two of you. Even a friendly breakup could be awkward, but worse it could hurt both people involved and leave bad feelings among fellow employees who were in on the matter and took sides.

*Sexual harassment involves something beyond natural overtones.* Sexual harassment in the workplace is behavior of a sexual nature that causes a coworker to be uncomfortable and has a negative impact on productivity. In most cases, sexual harassment is more than one isolated incident. Rather, it is behavior pursued in a deliberate way over a period of time.

There are three forms of harassment:

- **Verbal.**   Examples are telling risqué jokes, commenting on one's sexual anatomy, pursuing an unwanted relationship, and asking for sexual favors.

- **Visual.**   Examples are wearing suggestive attire, staring at someone's anatomy, flirting nonverbally, and sitting in a revealing position.

- **Physical.**   Examples are touching, standing too close, giving a "too lengthy" handshake, and excessive hugging.

Sexual harassment violates the law and inhibits work performance. Victims can be male or female, a manager or subordinate, a vendor or customer. When an individual believes she (or he) is being sexually harassed, the following steps are recommended: (1) take your complaint to your immediate supervisor; (2) provide the specifics and dates involved; (3) document any further harassment while waiting for the supervisor to correct the situation; (4) if further action is necessary, file a formal complaint with the director of human resources or a superior other than your immediate supervisor; (5) if the source of the harassment happens to be your supervisor, the first step should be to speak to her (or his) superior.

## Age Differences

The new employee who is young, capable, and ambitious is faced with a peculiar challenge in most organizations. And it doesn't take long for the challenge to occur. You hear it expressed in many ways:

"I could have had that last promotion if I had had more seniority."

"Everyone in this company has age, seniority, or experience beyond mine. I'll never get a chance. I'm wasting my time and ability. I won't get a chance to show what I can do until I'm thirty."

"I think I'll grow a mustache, so I'll at least appear older."

Many employees between the ages of eighteen and thirty consider their youth a handicap. Some feel that they must put in time to reach a certain age level before they will be given a chance to demonstrate their ability. In a few cases, the situation becomes aggravated because the employee appears younger than he (or she) actually is.

It is easy to appreciate having a youth-discrimination attitude if you put yourself in the place of a young employee. When she (or he) sees older, more experienced employees everywhere, she may begin to feel that the generation gap is wider inside a business organization than outside. Because she wants to make progress, wants to move, and doesn't want to wait, the pressure builds.

Yet, it is not unusual today to find young supervisors in charge of employees many years their senior. No doubt some young people have the human-relations skills to compensate for their youth. Take the cases of Laurel and Leonard as examples.

**Laurel.** Laurel manages a large fashion department in a major department store. The department had sales of over $1 million last year. Laurel, who just turned 20, supervises nine full-time people, all of whom are at least twice her age. The problems are constant and the pressure is great. But, without exception, the older workers consider her an excellent manager, and her boss feels she has a great future.

**Leonard.** Leonard, 23 years old with one year of college behind him, is the manager of a large, popular restaurant. Two of the three managers who work under him are much older than he, and one is old enough to be his father. In fact, most of the regular employees are older than Leonard. The establishment is open twenty-four hours a day, and the problems never end. Under all this pressure, Leonard still seems to be on top of everything. The president of the chain feels that Leonard is just getting started.

How do young people like Laurel and Leonard do it?

They demonstrate early that they can accept and handle responsibility. They demonstrate that they can make mature decisions. They demonstrate great personal confidence. But most of all, they demonstrate skills in human relations. They show that they can build strong MRT relationships with older and more experienced employees and management personnel, as well as with people their own age. The fact is that your more mature fellow workers will not resist your progress if you go about it in the right way. Rather, they will want you to succeed and will be willing to help you.

Your decision, then, is a simple one. If you are ambitious, you can either drift along until you are older and have more experience, or you can face the human-relations challenge now and speed up your progress. If you decide to make the effort, there are, among others, two important rewards you should provide in building a relationship with a more mature, experienced person.

*Everyone, regardless of age, likes to be noticed.* Older employees, especially, like to receive compliments (even if the compliments border on flattery). They like to feel that they are still important as employees and as people. They need to feel appreciated and respected. They like to receive credit when due.

*A more mature person often likes to keep a young image.* Any action that tends to make a mature person feel out of touch or out of date is a mistake. Try to make him (or her) feel that he still has a lot to offer, that he is part of today's world, not yesterday's. Make a big effort to keep the communication lines open at all times. Do not isolate yourself from this person. Seek his advice. Always include him in your plans for any job related social activities. Remember, you cannot expect a good vertical relationship with him—should you become his supervisor later on—unless you build a good horizontal working relationship with him now.

Perhaps the most important aspect of building good relationships with mature employees is learning how to gain their respect. Thus, demonstrate your ability, hard work, and reliability on a day-to-day basis. Deeds will do more than words. Statistics will do more than promises. Performance will do more than flattery.

More than anything else, learn from this person. Her (or his) additional years of experience have taught her many things that you can learn without having to experience them. You can learn through osmosis. Then, if the time comes for you to move ahead of her, give her credit for making it possible. Let her have the satisfaction of calling you her protégé. Let her take pride in your success.

It will be wise of you to keep your relationship on a formal basis until she gives you the signal to be more relaxed and personal.

What about reversing the situation? How can the mature worker build better relationships with the new, younger employee? There are many steps that can be taken. Here are three that will be greatly appreciated: (1) be patient with new employees' adjustment problems, (2) help them learn by sharing your experience with them, and (3) if needed, give them the confidence to communicate with you.

## Irritation Threshold

Relationships are frequently endangered because one of the individuals has an irritating habit or mannerism that bothers the other. Here are some common ones:

- Harsh or loud voice
- Irritating laugh
- Overbearing manner

- Constant name dropping
- Constant talk about money
- Constant reference to sex
- Telling dirty or unfunny stories
- Overuse of certain words or expressions
- Constant discussion of personal problems
- Constant bragging about their successes off the job or the successes of their children
- Having an opinion on everything
- Dominating conversations, especially in meetings

Whether or not a habit or mannerism becomes an irritant depends upon the threshold or *tolerance level* of the second party. If one party has a high enough threshold, he (or she) may not even notice something that might bother someone else. On the other hand, it is possible for an individual to have a very low threshold for a certain mannerism. In the case of a low tolerance threshold, the habit can do considerable damage to the relationship.

> **Diane.** Diane is an excellent example of a young employee who hurt her relationship with a few fellow workers because of a nervous giggle that followed almost every sentence she uttered. Unfortunately, Diane had no idea what was happening. She was not conscious of the habit or of the fact that it was hurting her relationships with certain people who had low irritation thresholds. One day, after getting a complaint from a good employee who worked next to Diane, the supervisor had a talk with Diane about her nervous giggle. Thanks to some very hard work on Diane's part, the irritating mannerism all but disappeared in a few weeks.

Once the individual knows about them, bad habits can usually be modified and sometimes eliminated. But the person at the other end of the relationship must not expect too much too soon. In some cases it may be necessary to learn to live with certain irritants by making an attempt to raise one's tolerance level. Seldom do such irritants come from only one side of the relationship. Almost all of us have at least a few mannerisms or habits that bother other people. The individual, even in the business environment, retains the right to remain pretty much the way he (or she) is. Some adjustment on your part to such factors will be necessary in most relationships. Tolerance, obviously, is a human relations skill that must be developed.

> *Your attitude, like the small flame of a candle, can have an illuminating effect.*

# Case 9

**"What's in it for me?"**

# Currency

When it comes to his career, Sam deals in only one currency, and that is money. Sam wants big bucks, and he wants them fast. Human relations and compassion (other forms of exchange) have no appeal to Sam.

You can read Sam's attitude in his movements. He appears totally confident, and he seems to know how to be aggressive at just the right time. As a result, many of his classmates envy him for the job opportunities that he is bound to have offered to him.

A quiet dissenter is Ralph. Ralph feels that money is important but that it comes to those who select careers that contribute to the lives of others as much as to those who take a direct megabucks approach. Ralph made this comment to Sam (a good friend of his) yesterday: "You're going to make it fast, Sam, but I think I will be happier getting to where I'm going. And, who knows, I might wind up with as much money as you while my personal values remain intact. I think you are sacrificing human-relations values for the dollar, and in real life this is not necessary."

Sam replied: "It's a jungle out there, Ralph. You may wind up as happy as I do. But you and your values will get pushed around so much that you will be sidelined as far as money is concerned. I can worry about values after I have it made!"

How would you reply if you were part of this conversation? Would you side with Sam or Ralph? How do you intend to maintain your personal values and still enjoy monetary success? (For a suggested answer, see page 228.)

# PART III

# Maximizing Your Relationships

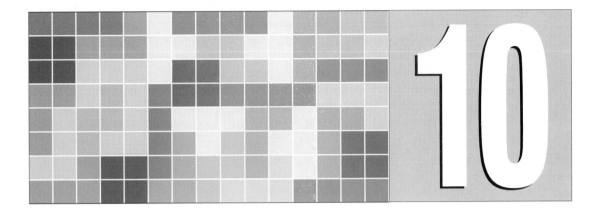

# Success as a Team Player

**"I cooperate with everybody."**

Thought for the Day: Believing in yourself and others is the best faith one can have to achieve realistic goals.

In the previous chapter we took a close look at the various elements often found *within* a working relationship. We gave recognition to the possible presence of value conflicts, sexual overtones, age differences, and ethnic implications. We introduced the mutual reward theory (MRT) as a way to build and maintain healthy relationships under all conditions.

*In this chapter, we focus on how these elements take on more importance for you as a member of a working team.*

In the typical traditional department, the supervisor is at the top of the pyramid.

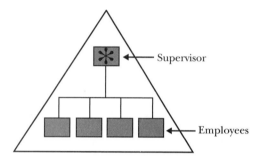

She (or he) manages or controls the operation from that position, assumes responsibility for results, hopefully welcomes suggestions, and often involves employees in decision making, but adheres to the philosophy that *most employees need frequent, steady supervision.*

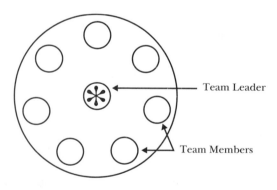

Under the team concept, the supervisor operates within the team itself.

He (or she) takes time to involve members in the formation of goals, delegates authority and considerable responsibility to the team, communicates frequently, and assumes that team members *like to manage themselves.*

Anyone who has participated in a team sport learns that success depends upon the contributions of all members. It is one for all and all for one. The pressure to produce comes more from other team members than from the coach. And, most important of all, is the *way individual members work together.* A good team member is anxious to make another member a star, providing that the team itself wins. MRT operates at a higher level in a successful team than it does in a traditional department.

The team concept in industry is more popular today than ever before. Literally there are volumes of books on the subject, and team-building seminars are prevalent all across the country. Many corporations are retraining traditional supervisors to become team leaders. Why all this emphasis? Because there is evidence that work teams often achieve greater productivity than traditional departments.

## Team Membership Essentials

As a team member or potential team member of the future, what should you learn so you will be an outstanding team player? Here are three basic requirements:

1. *A successful, highly respected team member should accept and promote the four Cs of team membership or your willingness to:*

   - *Conform* to all decisions made by team members.
   - *Cooperate* with other team members without undue conflict.
   - *Contribute* talents without holding back for selfish reasons.
   - *Collaborate* with another member on a creative idea regardless of who receives more recognition for success.

The four Cs of team membership communicate how team members can control their behavior so that all actions are in the best interest of the team as a whole. The four Cs of team membership also need to be accomplished with enthusiasm, self-discipline, and little supervision. It is not always easy to be a productive member of a work team. Some who have tried it prefer the traditional structure.

2. *To be effective, a team must have a leader who is sensitive to the needs of the team members.* It is the team leader who can create a working environment where everyone wants to contribute. That is, as a team member, you must understand the role of your team leader and give her (or him) your full support even when mistakes are made. If you complain about your leader, you may also be criticizing your team, which means you are criticizing yourself.

3. *Not all work environments are suitable for the team approach.* You may be preparing for a career where only parts of the team concept are applicable. For example, fast food operations may have such a frequent turnover of personnel there is not enough time to form a group into a team. In such cases, and many others, the traditional approach may produce the best results. In contrast, in a research department where a high level of creativity is needed, the team approach may be almost mandatory.

Each work environment and situation should be studied by management to determine which approach—the pyramid, the circle, or a blend of both—will produce the best results. Regardless of where you might wind up as an employee, the more you learn about *both* styles the better.

How would you rate yourself as a team member? Completing the exercise that follows may provide you with some insights.

---

### RATE YOURSELF AS A TEAM MEMBER

The purpose of this exercise is to give you an idea of just how good a team member you might become. Simply place a check mark in the appropriate square opposite each question and total your points at the end. Give an excellent rating 5 points, a good rating 3, and a weak score 1.

| Question | Excellent | Good | Weak |
|---|:---:|:---:|:---:|
| 1. How willing would you to accept the fact be that another team member might be stronger than you in a certain area? | ❏ | ❏ | ❏ |
| 2. What would be your chances of maintaining a more positive attitude in a team than working in a regular group or alone? | ❏ | ❏ | ❏ |
| 3. What would be your chances of quickly resolving a human conflict in which you are involved? | ❏ | ❏ | ❏ |
| 4. How good would you be at conforming, cooperating, and contributing when, in some cases, others may enjoy personal gain more than you? | ❏ | ❏ | ❏ |
| 5. What would be your patience threshold in working with a team member slower than yourself? | ❏ | ❏ | ❏ |
| 6. How receptive would you be toward a goal developed by your team when you hold a minority position? | ❏ | ❏ | ❏ |
| 7. How would you rate yourself in terms of working effectively with team members from ethnic groups different from your own? | ❏ | ❏ | ❏ |

| Question | Excellent | Good | Weak |
|---|---|---|---|
| 8. How understanding would you be of members with a point of view different from yours? | ❏ | ❏ | ❏ |
| 9. How well do you think you would accept a team leader who always takes time to see that all members participate in the decision-making process? | ❏ | ❏ | ❏ |
| 10. How successful do you think you might be in keeping your ego from getting in the way of full cooperation with the team? | ❏ | ❏ | ❏ |

TOTAL SCORE

If you scored 40 or more points, you show indications that you would be a sensitive and productive team member. You would probably like being on a team. If you scored between 30 and 40 points, you could probably adjust to team membership without great difficulty. If you scored below 30 points, you might be happier and more productive working in a traditional group or alone. And, since teamwork is so important in a productive business environment, it may be in your best interest to work on improving your "weak" areas.

## Membership on a Diverse Team

We often hear that the right combination of talent among a team of people, when everyone is working together, can produce a sum greater than the total of each individual operating alone. This is true. Teams that work in harmony (the best possible horizontal relationships) are those that win the awards. Also, teams made up of culturally diverse people frequently have broader perspectives than teams of employees who all have the same background.

Have you stopped to think about how culturally diverse your environment is? If you haven't, you may want to make some observations the next time you are standing in line on a campus, at a bank, at a fast-food restaurant, or at a post office waiting your turn. Recently for example, at a post office, a line with the following six people was observed: a young Latin American mother with a baby, a middle-aged African American male, an Anglo male teenager, an Asian American female, and an elderly East Indian male. While you may find your experience very different, what is described here is very commonplace in many geographical areas of the world.

Now, let's consider such a scenario as a work team. Note from the following graphic that there is a high cultural mix of team members among the females and males that make up this work group.

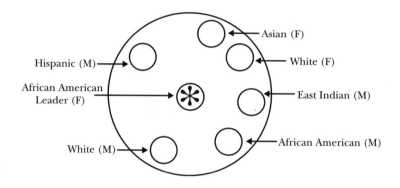

If you were to join this team, how comfortable would you be? What would you want to learn from the various members of this team?

Now assume, for a moment, that you are a team member, and a new individual from another culture is assigned to your team. How would you go about helping the new team member make the transition? What things might you do to help the new member become comfortable and contribute at a high level? Check those that fall within your comfort zone:

❏ Explain the meaning of some of the common slang expressions, jargon, or idioms in your culture and how they may differ from those of other cultures.

❏ In a sensitive way, explain why a mannerism in another person's culture may differ from yours (e.g., handshake vs. a hug).

❏ Discuss little things the newcomer can do to fit in and contribute to a team.

❏ Assist the individual in understanding how workers in your culture generally view leaders and supervisors. For example, explain when and how the newcomer should approach a leader for advice and guidance.

❏ Help a person understand business protocol where you work, and be generous in giving compliments when progress is made.

In assisting others, especially culturally diverse newcomers, to learn the work customs where you work, you will enrich your own life because new employees never forget those who give them a helping hand when they need it most. You should, however, be aware of some pitfalls in overidentifying with new members. Your primary goal should be to strengthen the team, not just to build an enjoyable relationship with a person who has an intriguing foreign background. Further, if you go too far, one of two things may happen. First, the newcomer may become overly dependent on you or may not foster relationships with others. Second, if you spend too much time with a new team member, you may turn other team members against you or against the new team member.

Although the application of MRT is a successful way to create and maintain harmonious relationships in any environment, its contribution to the success of a work team, when properly understood, can be exceptional. In may cases, work team rewards may be unevenly distributed at the beginning. But when the team wins, everything is balanced out. For example, a new team member may need to back up more experienced team members at the start, as in the case of Gregg.

> **Gregg.**   When Gregg was invited to join a special team with a great reputation within his company, he was excited. Experienced members were most helpful during his transition period. But it didn't take them long to discover that Gregg was more interested in his own ideas than listening to or helping others. As a result, he started to isolate himself.
>
> When a senior member of the team invited Gregg to lunch, it became obvious to Gregg that he had violated an important team rule. The team member explained it to Gregg this way. "Gregg, it is my understanding that you were on the varsity football team in college and that you played the position of guard when your team was in possession of the ball. In short, you did the blocking for your quarterback and for those who carried the ball. As a newcomer on our team, your primary job is to block for others by helping them with their ideas. This doesn't mean you can't carry the ball now and then. You can! And when it happens, others will block for you. Your big job at this point is to help the team become a winner. You see, when the team wins, everyone shares in the rewards. When this happens, it doesn't matter what position you played."

Sometimes new team members forget that when they have an idea that needs support from others, the kind of blocking they receive may depend upon the quality of blocking they did for others when they were new to the team. In the long run, MRT works.

## Team Attitude Factors

Success as a team member depends heavily upon the attitude of the individual toward the team. All teams are different. They may work on creative matters, production, service, and so on, but no team can function at its highest level if even one member has a consistently negative attitude.

Regardless of the type of team, its composition, and its leadership, there are attitude factors that must be present among all team members. Here are a few.

■ *Enthusiastic acceptance of the team concept as an organizational form.* If you support such ideas as supervising yourself and working unselfishly for the team, you do so not because you are expected to contribute your best, but because you want to do your best.

■ *Accepting the four Cs (conforming, cooperating, contributing, and collaborating) of team membership.* As a team member, you will achieve because you will achieve more for your firm than would be true if you were an independent worker.

■ *Undertaking the responsibility of self-discipline.* By self-disciplining yourself, you recognize that your team leader has a less demanding style than would be the case in a traditional department.

■ *Keeping your own attitude positive and upbeat.* Your good attitude will help your other team members to be positive. Team spirit can do wonders for productivity.

■ *Being willing to put your career temporarily in the hands of the team.* Your future is somewhat determined by how other team members perform. Many a professional sports star has had a modest career because he (or she) was a member of a nonwinning team.

■ *Realizing that the contributions of other team members may be different from yours.* It is the blending of talent and abilities that can give a team power.

■ *Maintaining an open attitude toward people of diverse cultures.* An unprejudiced attitude toward all team members, regardless of cultural and other differences, is essential for effective teamwork.

■ *Realizing that a good team leader has some of the attributes of a successful coach.* Your attitude toward your team leader—a key individual—is crucial.

Anyone who has been a member of a sports team of any kind probably has some valuable insights into what makes a work team successful. The more these insights are applied, the better. The comparison, however, can only go so far. Sports teams operate for only one season; then they can start over, with some new members and a built-in goal of winning a conference. A work team, on the other hand, does not have the luxury of starting over frequently. Not only that, but an organizational team must create goals from within and provide its own rewards. The thrill of winning, however, can be equally satisfying.

> *Attitude is the rock upon which the foundation of team spirit is built.*

# Case 10

**"I treat everyone as an individual."**

# Controversy

Justine and Zeke are two of the most vocal students in the organizational communication class. Although other members make significant contributions during discussions, everyone, including the professor, enjoys it when Justine and Zeke square off on controversial topics. Take yesterday as an example.

Justine stated that the essence of good human relations is to treat everyone as a separate and unique individual. "Each person deserves the same high level of treatment and respect given to others. It really doesn't matter about ethnic origin, religious preferences, sex, age, or education. All we need do is to accept this one basic principle, and the world will immediately become a better place. What do you do if after giving a person fair and dignified treatment, he scorns you? Well, you can turn your cheek once or twice and then politely back away without changing your basic attitude. It is *continuing* the way you look at people from the start that counts."

Zeke replies in a quiet, patient voice. "I think it is wonderful that Justine is an idealist and believes that the more we treat people as individuals, never grouping them together, the better. But Justine's idea that one basic premise will change the world is simplistic. What we really need to do is evaluate people on their performance as producers and human beings, not on the color of their skin or background. It is what people do that is important, not what they look like or the way they dress. The real criterion is to treat people as individuals based upon what they are doing to make the world a better place for all of us."

Assume that you would like to add a few sentences to either Justine's or Zeke's comments. What would you say? (For a suggested answer, see page 229.)

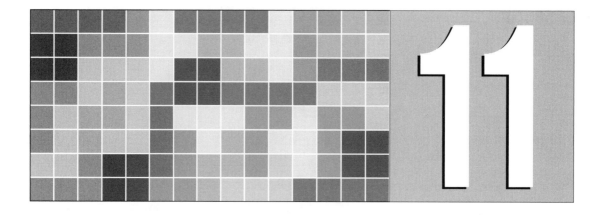

# Stress Management: Releasing Your Frustrations Harmlessly

**"1 2 3 4 5 6 . . ."**

Thought for the Day: Permitting yourself to get upset, frustrated, angry, or aggressive is a condition that only you control.

Minimizing the stress in your life undoubtably will contribute to your overall well being and happiness. Because it is possible to learn techniques to manage your stress, it is a popular belief that stress reduction is inversely proportional to maintaining a positive attitude. That is, as your stress levels go down, your attitude becomes better. If you can identify and understand the elements that are causing your stress, and if you take appropriate action, you should be better able to avoid burnout. This chapter will introduce you to the frustration-aggression hypothesis, an idea that can greatly assist you in understanding your own behavior and that of others.

## Frustration

Everyone encounters frustrations in life. We learn to adjust to most of them easily without hurting our relations with others. Sometimes, however, a major frustration or series of frustrations may cause our feelings to boil to the point where we lash out verbally and seriously injure or destroy a relationship we deeply treasure.

Naturally, many disturbing experiences occur on the job. In fact, most of your frustrations may be job oriented. The mechanic who climbs under a car to do a repair job, only to discover that he (or she) took the wrong wrench with him, becomes frustrated. A supervisor who must get a report in before going home to an important dinner engagement must cope with feelings of frustration.

*Frustration is the feeling of disturbance or anxiety you experience when you meet a temporary block to your immediate goal.*

The more important the goal is to you, the more intense is the disturbance. Major frustrations come about when something happens to keep you from reaching a goal that means a lot to you. While small frustrations can usually be eliminated quickly, major frustrations must often be controlled for days or weeks before an adjustment can be made. Controlling major frustrations may mean replacing one goal with another.

## Aggression

Now we must ask ourselves the big question: What happens when we become frustrated?

*Almost always, frustration leads to aggressive behavior.* When a steam boiler builds up too much pressure inside, some of the steam must be released. If there is no safety valve, the boiler will explode. Just as the steam boiler must release some of the pressure after it reaches a certain point, so must the individual. When a person releases pressure, it is usually in some form of aggressive behavior.

Take the case of the driver who becomes frustrated when he (or she) meets a slow-moving car on the highway. He may curse (verbal aggression) and drive on. Or he may pound his horn and speed around the slow car (physical aggression). Or it could disturb him so much that when he returns to his office he may refuse to speak to his assistant or co-workers (passive aggression).

*Aggression takes many forms.* Physical aggression, especially if it involves another person, is serious. It can be assault and battery and could mean a police record. Verbal aggression can also get a person into serious trouble. Telling off a fellow worker or supervisor at the wrong time and place can destroy a relationship and cripple a person's progress.

*Learn to release aggression in acceptable ways without hurting relationships with others.* There are acceptable forms of physical aggression. There are acceptable forms of verbal aggression.

A parent might become frustrated because of her (or his) small children. She could act out the aggression that follows the frustration by punishing one child with a very harsh slap in the face. Hitting another person, however, is an unacceptable release of aggression. On the other hand, if the parent released her aggression physically, by energetically shampooing the carpets or mowing the lawn, and then disciplined the child in some other manner, it would be more acceptable. If the parent takes out her aggression on the carpets or lawn—not on the child—she has found a good release for her aggression.

## Releasing Tension

There are many acceptable ways a person can release inner tension due to frustrations. Here are a few.

| On the Job | Off the Job |
|---|---|
| Take a walk | Prepare an exotic meal |
| Talk things over with a third party | Clean out the garage |
| Do some disagreeable paperwork | Play golf or go running |

Sometimes just by doing something physical we release inner tensions, and no one is hurt. It is usually more difficult to find acceptable ways to release inner tensions on the job than it is off the job.

If a worker became frustrated on the job and picked a fight with a fellow worker, he (or she) would demonstrate an unacceptable release of aggression. If, on the other hand, he walked away and slammed a door where nobody could hear it, he would be releasing his aggression in an acceptable manner. He *could* hurt his human relationships, however, by slamming a door in *front* of others. Others might interpret the action as a display of temper or immaturity.

As a mature, mentally healthy person, you must seek and find acceptable releases for your inner aggression. You should conduct yourself in such a manner so as to eliminate many of the frustrations of life. The fewer frustrations you have, the fewer times you will have to seek acceptable releases.

But you cannot eliminate all frustrations from life. You should expect to find it necessary to release your anxiety feelings occasionally. It is not always healthy for a person to keep her (or his) tensions bottled up. Some release is necessary and healthy. You would do well, however, to refrain from any kind of verbal aggression on the job. It would be wiser to unburden yourself to someone you can trust outside the organization—your spouse or a good friend.

To help you to understand the importance of the frustration-aggression hypothesis, read the following story about Alice, an intelligent, highly motivated person who let stress affect her life.

> **Alice.**   A well-educated young person, Alice joined a large utility company as a management trainee. She liked her job, and for two years her productivity and human relations were very good. She took advantage of every opportunity to learn. She received four salary increases.
>
> One day, in talking to the director of human resources, Alice mentioned that she would like to qualify as an employment interviewer. The director, pleased with her success so far, encouraged her. He told Alice that she would be considered if an opportunity came along. Alice, more highly motivated than ever, continued to do an outstanding job and set her goal for the next opening as an interviewer.
>
> Two weeks later, another person was promoted to the position of interviewer. Alice was not informed about the change. Not thinking that the plans for the personnel change might have been set before her initial talk with the director, Alice permitted herself to become deeply frustrated. She had set a goal for herself, and now they had selected another person.
>
> "At least they could have talked to me!"
> "Why should that person get the breaks?"
> "So that's the way they keep their promises!"

Alice, without thinking it through, permitted her frustration to grow. Indeed, she set out to feed it by talking it over with a few fellow employees, which only intensified her feelings.

What happened?

Alice released her frustrations through verbal aggression. For the first time in her career, she sounded off in a highly emotional manner at a weekly staff meeting. She voiced more than her share of gripes during coffee breaks. And all of this found its way back to the department of human resources. The result was what you might expect: Alice, through her verbal aggression, had hurt her previously excellent relationships with others. Six months later, another position as an interviewer opened up, and Alice was passed over.

What should Alice have done from the outset of her frustration until she learned the reason why she didn't get the promotion?

Alice should have released her aggressive behavior outside her job until she discovered or rationally sought out the truth of the situation. She could have spent more time playing her favorite sport or talking her problem over with a close friend. Or she could have vented her frustration by putting it into writing without showing it to others, a mechanism that seems to help a number of people. None of these actions would have injured her relations with others.

## Avoid Self-Victimizing

We must all learn to live with frustrating experiences without becoming verbally aggressive on the job, without damaging our relations with others, and *without victimizing ourselves.*

Aggressive behavior resulting from inner disturbances and hostilities takes many strange forms. It's not always physical or verbal. It may be passive. In extreme cases, passive aggression takes the form of silence. Deliberate silence. Planned silence.

Silence on the part of the person who has been frustrated is a most potent weapon. Nothing is more uncomfortable to your fellow workers than your silence. Nothing destroys relations faster. No one can interpret your silence. All anyone can do is to leave you alone and wait. But it is uncomfortable for them, and productivity suffers.

When a person takes out his (or her) inner aggressive feelings in silence, who is on the receiving end? Fellow employees? The supervisor? Although everyone suffers from silence of this nature, the silent person himself suffers the most. He is, in fact, taking out his aggressive feelings on himself. It is a form of self-victimization. Naturally, self-victimization is most destructive to the human personality. It is also juvenile. Many normal, mature people, however, temporarily react to a series of frustrations in this manner.

## The Hypothesis in Practice

It is hoped that the preceding discussion has given you a good understanding of the frustration-aggression hypothesis. To summarize, how can you put the frustration-aggression idea to work for you?

1. *Admit that your frustrations often produce aggressive behavior of some kind and learn to recognize them.* Once you recognize the frustrations that cause your aggressive behavior, you should work on ways to channel aggressive actions into acceptable outlets. Be careful to release your aggressions in the right way and in the right place. Keep from releasing them on the job in a way that will hurt relationships and your future.

2. *Recognize aggressive behavior in others (including executives).* Keep in mind that aggressive action by others is usually not directed toward you per-

sonally. You may just happen to be at the wrong place at the wrong time and the best available target for verbal abuse. You should try to accept such behavior as a natural outcome of uncontrollable frustrations and not overreact to it. An accepting attitude should make for all around better human understanding. As a result, your relationships with people who express their aggression probably will not suffer as much as if you were neither aware nor sensitive to the factors which prompted their frustration-aggresion behaviors.

3. *Be sensitive to your own verbal aggression, and be very cautious in group discussions and staff meetings.* When you need to release feelings verbally, do so to a friend outside the company and not to a fellow employee, thus protecting your work relationships.

4. *Don't let aggressive behavior keep you from reaching your ultimate goal.* When a detour is necessary, you should take it. When an unexpected block to your plans appears, accept it for what it is. If frustration occurs, release it in an acceptable way and come up with an alternative goal. Do not allow aggressive behavior to victimize you on a permanent basis.

## Corporate Aggression

Another form of aggression—aggression toward your company—can be subtle and sinister. Aggression on the part of an employee toward the company for which he (or she) works has been the downfall of many career-minded persons. There is rarely anything personal about such a person's aggressive behavior. Such a person seems to get along well enough with fellow workers and immediate supervisors. Instead, the aggression always seems to be directed toward the company itself. It isn't just the top brass or middle management. It is the company. The employee often seems to hold his present plight (lack of progress or of personal adjustment to life) against the company.

In a very real sense, it is frustrating to work in any organization. Some rules must be followed. Some degree of conformity is expected. Some loss of individuality is usually necessary. Some people, however, seem to nurse their minor frustrations into one major hang-up against the organization itself. When aggression build up is permitted to happen, aggressive action of serious proportions frequently develops. The employee begins to fight a hypothetical monster that seems to be controlling her (or his) life without giving the person a chance to change. Often one hears expressions like these from such an individual:

"This organization does nothing but chew people up and spit them out."

"This company is so large that the only thing that keeps us from getting lost altogether is the computer."

"I'd put in for a transfer, but by the time it got through channels I'd be ready to retire."

It is counterproductive to direct one's aggressive behavior toward a large corporate structure. In the first place, these organizations are usually too large. Second, when a person attacks the company, she (or he) starts to lose loyalty to it. *And it begins to show in the employee's attitude*—not overnight, of course, but in subtle ways that begin to hurt that person's progress in the company.

## Stress Anecdote

Stress can be viewed as the fever that comes with overwork, trying to reach too many goals at the same time, and working with difficult peers and superiors. When you learn to release your frustrations harmlessly, you are lowering the fever by reducing the stress that has accumulated within you. For example, assume that you build the stress within you to a level where action is required. What do you do? You release the stress through some form of activity, recreation, or just getting away for a short time. Releasing stress lowers the fever. Then, by rebuilding yourself physically (through more activity), you also recover your positive attitude. In other words, one answer to burnout is managing stress by releasing your frustrations without having to cut back on your productivity.

In summary, this chapter has attempted to show you why you should try to release your frustrations harmlessly. Its purpose has been to help you avoid self-victimization so you maintain the positive, productive relationships that will further, not hinder, your career progress.

> *A positive attitude is the enemy of stress and frustration.*

# Case 11

**"Me and my big mouth!"**

# Frustration

As Allen thinks about the last two years of his life, it makes him angry. He's tired all of the time; in fact, it's a chore just to get up in the morning. He is bored with his programming job and he despises his Ms. Know-It-All boss. His co-workers aren't any better. And friends? Of course, he doesn't have any, thanks to his bitter divorce.

While riding the train to work, Allen thinks about what he'll do after work—that makes him angry too since he'll rush home and probably have to discipline his two kids for their falling grades, not doing their chores, etc. Miring down in self-pity about how things can't get worse, the little girl leaning over the seat in front of him spills her orange juice on his suit. That's it! He immediately jumps up and yells at the child and mother. The little girl starts crying and even though the mother is very apologetic, Allen continues to give them both a piece of his mind—not an unusual behavior these days for Allen.

When the little girl cries "I want my Grandma," tears welt up in the mother's eyes. The mother, looking extremely sad as if the weight on her shoulders is very heavy, tries to console her daughter. What Allen doesn't know is that the Grandmother passed away last week and the little girl had been living with her Grandmother for the past six months while the mother was recuperating from surgery.

Was Allen justified in his outburst (with or without knowing the situation of the mother and little girl)? Besides his divorce, what is "growing" Allen's frustration? What can he do to get into a better frame of mind and reduce his stress? (For a suggested answer, see page 229.)

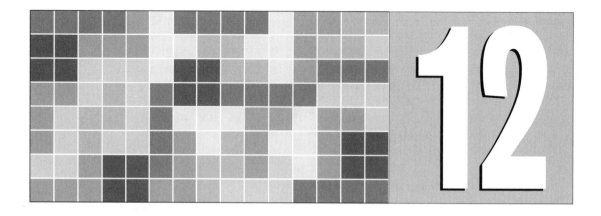

# Restoring Injured Relationships

**"Some relationships are not worth saving."**

Thought for the Day: Negative thoughts and actions are like toxic waste. Unless they are recycled into something positive, they can be detrimental to you and to everyone around you.

No matter how skillful one becomes at building healthy and rewarding human relationships, such relationships can easily be damaged through insensitivity and misunderstanding by either party. Human relationships are fragile. Once an injury occurs, the restoration process can be like walking on glass barefooted; it can be difficult—even challenging—but not impossible.

In the work environment, damages occur when there is a misuse of power by leaders, when the behavior of one person toward another is less than honest, when there are breakdowns in communications, and for a host of other reasons, many of which are highly personal and unintended. The important thing to remember is that *all* relationships—both on and off the job—occasionally become damaged and need repairing.

## Make Repairs Quickly

When a relationship is in need of repair work and nothing is done about it, everyone loses. That is why it could be to your advantage to initiate restoration *even when you are not primarily responsible for the injury.*

> **June.**    Without intending to do so, June let her emotions spill over last Friday and became testy with Grace, her favorite co-worker. Grace, wounded emotionally, reacted with a huffy silence for the rest of the day. June worried about that situation all weekend but failed to make repairs Monday. Early Tuesday, Grace initiated a discussion on the incident that gave June an opportunity to apologize, and the relationship was restored. Although she was not at fault, Grace was not content to work under an uncomfortable climate, so she used her human-relations skills to restore the relationship.

> **Gilbert.**    Last week Gilbert came down too hard on Harry over a minor work rule infraction. Harry, knowing Gilbert (his supervisor) would find it difficult to apologize, took action himself. On the following day he said: "Gilbert, our relationship is important to me, so I want to keep communication lines open and eliminate any differences that may occur between us. I want to be relaxed and comfortable under your supervision. Is it a deal?"

Unfortunately, when a minor falling out between two people occurs, both parties may have a desire to nurse the hurt and pull further away from each other. If an injured relationship is allowed to continue, some dangerous side effects may develop. For example, the possibility exists that the relationship between them may become more toxic and spill over into bad relationships with others.

> **Jill.**    The rift that developed between Jill and Jessie pushed Jill into a negative rut. Some of Jill's other relationships also seemed to turn sour with Jill's negative change in attitude. Jill started to ask herself such questions as: "Why should I work hard to build healthy relationships when others could care less?" "Why should I permit myself to be vulnerable to the hurts of others carelessly imposed upon me?" Unfortunately, the road selected by

Jill was to withdraw into her newly designed shell and become less of a team member on the job and less socially accepted in her personal world. Jill had made the classic human-relations mistake of permitting a repairable rift to develop into a major problem.

If communication is the lifeblood of any relationship (see Chapter 9), then reopening communication lines should be the first step in restoring relationships. Which party initiates the communication is unimportant. Communication, in this sense, can be compared to using ointment to help heal a cut. The ointment (communication) by itself may not solve the problem, but it enhances the healing process. If neither party is willing to supply or apply the ointment, the wound may fester and eventually destroy the relationship.

Regardless of who may be at fault (often both parties are responsible), it is an effective human-relations practice to restore the relationship *as soon as possible.* Any lapse of time may seem to deaden the pain, but it can make restoration more difficult—and sometimes impossible. And those who move from one job to another, leaving a wake of broken relationships behind them, often pay a high price in many directions. Consider the following possibilities and consequences of not repairing quickly a damaged relationship:

- *Constructive "mind time" is lost.* Preoccupation with a relationship left unrepaired is self-defeating. Living day in and day out with an unhealthy relationship, especially with a supervisor, causes you to mentally reprocess the conflict over and over, thus stealing your "mind time" from more constructive pursuits. Those who permit conflict preoccupation to happen, often put their career progress on hold or in jeopardy.

- An *already stressful situation is compounded.* Emotional conflicts in the workplace can be more stressful than long hours, heavy concentration on a special project, or other heavy job demands. Worst of all, emotional stress makes everything else more difficult. To maintain peace of mind and high personal productivity, restoration of broken relationships should receive top priority. When not given immediate attention, false inferences often compound the stress. Statistics continue to tell us that over 50 percent of all resignations come from unsolved human conflicts.

- *Chances of becoming a victim increase.* In some work environments, a broken relationship left unattended can convert you into a victim. For example, a co-worker with whom you previously enjoyed a healthy relationship suddenly begins to fear you may replace him (or her). As a result, this individual deliberately creates a conflict situation in the hope that you will be unable to deal with it effectively. If the supervisor does not step in as a mediator/counselor and you refuse to take action yourself, you could easily wind up a victim. Your refusal to take action (even going to the supervisor with the problem) could give the co-worker the upper hand he seeks, and eventually management could misinterpret the situation in favor of the other employee. Your failure to remove the feeling of fear through communication and restore the relationship to its previous state could cause you to become a victim.

Such possibilities, although remote, should motivate you to set the difficult goal of creating, maintaining, and repairing relationships, even when you would prefer to ignore the individuals involved or to carry out a vendetta against them. In many cases, your career may depend upon how effective you are in practicing good human relations skills.

## Basic Repair Principles

There are four principles or guideposts that may assist you in repairing a damaged relationship.

1. *See the connection between repairing relationships and career success.* A damaged relationship left unrepaired between you and a co-worker or superior may reduce support you need at a later date. As a result, your upward mobility may be impeded. You have victimized yourself.

2. *Try to see behind the cause of the falling out.* When one takes the time to study the causes of breaks in human relationships, it becomes obvious that often one party was under unusual pressure, which precipitated the rift. It is easier to forgive when such causes can be identified. Through your own perception, try to see behind misunderstandings. Once you see why misunderstandings occur, your attitude toward rebuilding damaged relationships may be more positive.

3. *Develop a willingness to rebuild damaged relationships.* The more you nurse a resentment, the less effective you are in restoring a relationship. Some give-and-take from both sides is usually necessary for a satisfactory repair job. If one person is unwilling to listen, the process may never get off the ground. That is why some relationships are never repaired. Until you reach a point where your mind is open to the possibility of repair (regardless of who did the damage), you have not reached the effective level of *willingness.*

4. *Design your own rebuilding techniques.* As you ponder just *how* you might initiate a rebuilding process, many questions will emerge. Can both people save face? If hostility and resentment are present,

can they be dissipated through open communication so that the repair job is permanent? As you consider such factors, ask yourself these additional questions:

- Can you insert some humor into your approach?
- Can you be a better listener than a talker?
- Can you "give" as much as you expect from the other person?
- Can you forgive a little white lie so that the other person can save face?

## Relationship Rebuilding Strategies

Are you willing to state openly that the relationship is important to you—important enough to forgive and forget what or who caused the damage?

Once you feel your "willingness factor" is sufficient, consider these rebuilding strategies:

*Rebuilding strategy 1: If you were fully or partially responsible for the damage, swallow your pride and take the direct approach.* Say you are sorry and state: "I would like to get our relationship back to its previous healthy state as soon as possible. You and our relationship are important to me, and I intend to be more sensitive in the future."

We all make human-relations mistakes. We always will. Unless we accept the premise that now and then we need to initiate a repair job, we will lose many significant relationships well worth keeping.

*Rebuilding strategy 2: If you were not responsible for the damage, give the responsible person some room to make repairs.* That is, when the person at the other end of the relationship line makes the mistake (the reason is not important), give the person the opportunity to approach you to restore the relationship. Be accessible! Have an open mind! If the other person does not approach you in a reasonable length of time, take the initiative yourself. Taking the first step may sound like asking too much, but keep in mind that you may be getting hurt more than the person responsible. Why should you become a victim? Why not restore the relationship for *your* benefit? One way to employ strategy 2 is to say:

"That incident last week really got to me, Jack, and I'm bringing it up for discussion so that hopefully it won't happen again. If we don't work harder at maintaining our relationship, we will both wind up losers."

*Rebuilding strategy 3: When no one is clearly responsible for a rift, initiate a MRT (mutual reward theory) discussion so that the rewards both people receive from the relationship can be reviewed.* A MRT approach can help each person recognize how important the relationship has been in the past and can continue to be in the future. Only when rewards are somewhat equal do both people come out ahead. The win-win premise is the significance and the promise of MRT.

## Risk Factors

Restoring a damaged relationship involves risks. You may, for example, gather up your courage in a sincere effort to restore an important relationship, only to be rebuffed for your initiative.

> **Howard.**   After two days of increased silence and tension on the job, Howard approached his boss, Erin, to reconcile a communications misunderstanding. Erin responded by walking away. However, the following morning, Erin invited Howard to lunch with her, and the relationship was fully restored. With time to think over Howard's gesture, Erin had a change of attitude. The risk had been worth taking after all.

*Some people refuse to restore a relationship even if the alternative means finding a new job.* Yet the challenge of relationship restoration can be rich and rewarding. At times, the challenge of restoring a relationship can even give your career a needed boost.

In conclusion, keep in mind that a professional technician needs just the right tool to repair a sensitive instrument. The right tool to repair a damaged relationship is communication—in fact, it is the only tool available. When you use communication in a sensitive manner, you will be more than pleased with all of your relationship repair jobs.

> *If your present attitude were broadcast in stereo surround sound, how would you be received?*

# Case 12

**"I'm willing if you are."**

# Restoration

Noreen and Crystal are highly competent supervisors. They both possess out-standing computer skills, do quality work, and receive high productivity from their employees. There is only one problem. As supervisors, they must work closely together, and *they do not get along well with each other.*

Noreen is a single, highly competitive and assertive person who presents a "flashy and trendy" appearance. She sets a fast pace, and as far as management can tell, those who work in her section accept her leadership with enthusiasm. Crystal, on the other hand, is a family-oriented person with two children; she has a far more conservative approach to her job and lifestyle. Although her approach and management style are different from Noreen's, Crystal also gains high productivity from her staff.

Mrs. Ruby, their superior, is tired of the many personal conflicts that arise between Noreen and Crystal. She is fearful that they are drawing so much attention to their conflict that the productivity of her division (she has nine supervisors under her control) will suffer. Yesterday she called both of them into her private office and stated: "I respect both of you and appreciate your contributions, but it is obvious to everyone that your personal conflict is beginning to disturb the productivity of my division. I'm giving you three hours for lunch today compliments of our division. For the good of everyone, resolve your conflict and be back here at three o'clock to tell me what progress you have made. If you can't work it out, I will assist one of you in getting a transfer to another division."

What are the chances of the plan working? Will they resolve their differences? (Compare your ideas with those of the authors on page 229.)

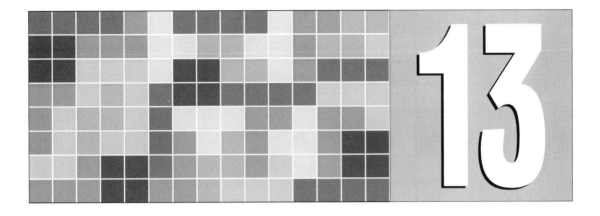

# Attitudes Among Culturally Diverse Co-Workers

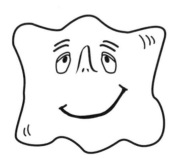

**"The more diversification the better."**

Thought for the Day: If you can't honestly expose the dialog you have with yourself, maybe you need to make some serious adjustments in your thinking.

Living in a culturally diverse environment has become a vitally important aspect of today's society. The United States, in particular, has become a culture of people bonded together by ethnic backgrounds as well as values, attainments, beliefs, and traditions (refer to discussion in Chapter 9). Similarly, as a department or a corporation integrates employees into the workplace, a "culture" of its own eventually develops.

## Your Cultural Comfort Zone

What is your attitude toward cultural diversification? Will you be comfortable working with more and more co-workers from cultures other than your own? To give you an indication, complete the following scale.

| CULTURAL DIVERSIFICATION COMFORT ZONE SCALE | | |
|---|---|---|
| Place a check mark in the appropriate square and total your answers at the end of the scale. | | |
| | **Yes** | **No** |
| 1. Do you sometimes unknowingly favor co-workers from one culture over another? | ☐ | ☐ |
| 2. Do you find yourself spending more social time during breaks and lunch periods with co-workers from your own culture? | ☐ | ☐ |
| 3. Do you give full acceptance to new employees from one culture more slowly than another? | ☐ | ☐ |
| 4. Would you feel unmotivated and at a disadvantage if for the first time a new supervisor was from a different culture than your own? | ☐ | ☐ |
| 5. When working near co-workers from other cultures, are you outwardly "cool" but inwardly resentful? | ☐ | ☐ |
| 6. Do you find that co-workers who have trouble with the English language irritate you? | ☐ | ☐ |
| 7. Are you less tolerant with co-workers who maintain aspects of their own cultures than those who fully adopt your culture? | ☐ | ☐ |

|  | Yes | No |
|---|:---:|:---:|
| 8. If you needed a co-worker to take your place while on a vacation, would you prefer to train someone from your own culture? | ❏ | ❏ |
| 9. Would those who know you best say you need more time to be fully free of cultural prejudice? | ❏ | ❏ |
| 10. Do you think it is more difficult for you to accept co-workers from a different culture than it is for them to accept you? | ❏ | ❏ |

TOTAL ☐ ☐

The more "No" answers you gave yourself, the more comfortable it should be for you to work in a culturally diverse workplace. However, you may wish to go back over the questions to see how many "Yes" answers you could, with effort, move into the "No" column. This exercise may give you some idea of how easy or difficult it may be for you to work effectively with a more diverse cultural mix of workers in the future.

We have learned that it is not only what you produce yourself, but how well you work with others that determines how much you contribute to your organization. And your contribution, no doubt, is significantly impacted by your attitude.

## Attitude Adjustment

What might you do to improve your attitude toward *all* co-workers regardless of cultural background? Here are three suggestions:

1. *As a permanent employee, take the initiative to build equally good relationships with all co-workers—especially those who are new and from a culture different than your own.* Go about building relationships slowly. Translated, this means you should play the role of the friendly, helpful host, but not to the extent that you might put your relationships with your regular co-workers in jeopardy.

   **Shirley.** Shirley is extremely friendly and outgoing. In fact, when a new employee arrives in her department she tries so hard to build a warm and friendly relationship that she makes it uncomfortable for the new arrival. Why is this? Because the new employee wants to win acceptance from *all* members of the team; and, if Shirley dominates her orientation, other employees may withdraw somewhat. You might even hear other employees say: "There goes Shirley again, trying to be a one-person welcoming committee."

Try to be a comfortable co-worker to know, but do not move too fast. Give the new employee a chance to adjust slowly and build equally good relationships with all team members.

2. *Give those from different cultures the opportunity to demonstrate their special talents.* Nothing will make new workers feel more comfortable than to win acceptance through their own performance. Their greatest need is to know that they can contribute. It is natural that newcomers in a work team or department feel shy or reluctant to express their special talents.

**Sue Lin.**   Sue Lin was raised and educated in Korea where she acquired unusually high computer skills. When Sue Lin took her first job in the United States, she decided, however, to soft-pedal her skills until she found a high degree of personal acceptance. Fortunately for Sue Lin, her team leader knew of her special abilities and brought them into play in a sensitive manner so that Sue Lin was able to win acceptance based on her skills as well as her personal qualities.

**Ramona.**   A large Canadian investment firm recruited Ramona from Mexico City immediately upon her university graduation. In addition to her accounting degree, she had unusual artistic talent that would be helpful to the advertising department. Her bilingual communication skills would be particularly effective with the company's growing market of Mexican customers. Because Ramona's supervisor did not bother to identify Ramona's strengths and talents, he assigned her to dull work tasks. As a result, her co-workers underestimated the contribution she could make. Had it not been for Jeanne, who made a special effort to know Ramona and discover her background, Ramona might have become discouraged and left the company.

Obviously, when a new employee becomes a member of a work team, adjustments must be made by all members of the team. If the work setting is not culturally diverse, a new employee from a culture other than the dominant culture of the team may offer additional challenges for everyone.

For example, let's assume that you work in a department where three cultures have already formed a highly productive team. The team, made up of mostly males who are African American, Anglo, and Hispanic, have molded together into a single productive unit with little evidence of cultural conflict or disharmony. Then, for the first time, an energetic young Japanese woman is introduced as a new team member. While we, regardless of our cultural background, have already made the adjustment, the new Japanese woman must, in effect, adjust to *three* different cultures—as well as to our predominently male team. Our challenge is much easier than that of the newcomer.

**3.** *Apply the mutual reward theory (MRT).* Mutual reward means that both individuals benefit from a relationship. The more equally the rewards balance out, the stronger and more permanent the relationship becomes. The MRT performs best when each participant is from a different culture because each person has more to learn from each other than probably could be gained from a less diverse relationship.

> **Jahal.**   After being educated in India, Jahal went to England to work for an export business—a firm eager to expand the market for their products in Jahal's native country. Initially, Jahal was very uncomfortable in the strange environment. Nearly a month passed before he felt at home and was willing to contribute ideas. Much of this was due to Sonja, a co-worker in the marketing department, who tutored Jahal in British marketing concepts. When the marketing director decided to send Jahal on a promotional trip back to India, Sonja was invited to go along; and Jahal had the opportunity to repay Sonja for her training. As a result, both employees came out ahead, and the win-win philosophy of the mutual reward theory came strongly into play.

Nothing erases differences and prejudices faster than two people from different cultures who build a strong working relationship between themselves. Sooner or later the rewards balance out.

## Mutual Understanding

We do not always recognize our own prejudices toward those from cultures different from our own. Sometimes, the only way to eliminate such prejudices is to get to know and understand each other by working closely over a long period of time.

> **Fernand.**   When Fernand went to work for a furniture company right out of high school, he had a real drive to achieve. It took him only two years to work himself up from a warehouse worker to the top delivery person. Fernand seemed to get along well with everyone. Then came the day his assistant, also of Philippino descent, resigned and Cedric, an African American, was assigned to him. Immediately, Fernand recalled the many fights between the two cultures in high school and figured he might have a challenge ahead of him. Cedric also was nervous about having a Philippino boss, wondering if he would receive fair and equitable treatment.
>
>      How did the relationship turn out? For a month there was little communication, but slowly the two came to know and understand each other's culture. Fernand talked a lot about his family. Cedric talked about his interest in sports and why he was going to college at night. Eventually, a strong relationship developed. When Fernand was given a promotion to the head of the shipping department, he strongly recommended Cedric as his replacement. The fears based upon old high school conflicts had dissipated, and a mutually rewarding relationship had been built.

Cultural attitudes are mental sets for or against those of a diverse cultures. Often they are biases created from family values or information transmitted by the media. Many people have negative mind sets against another culture when they have never had the opportunity to work closely with a person from that culture.

For example, if an individual who has English as a primary language has been raised to stereotype everyone from Mexico as weak in English skills, then that person needs to "exchange places" in her (or his) thinking. Also, she should try to build a close relationship with a person of Mexican descent who has excellent English skills. Similarly, if an individual has stereotyped women in the work force to be less capable than men or has characterized a specific culture as unwilling to accept work responsibilities, then the individual needs to seek out work relationships that dispel these stereotypes. A good way to eliminate your stereotyped feelings is to put yourself in the other person's place. Ask yourself how you would feel if you were characterized by your co-workers as having poor communication or human-relations skills; being inflexible, pompous, or aloof; or being lazy and unhelpful—just because of a cultural bias they may have.

## Cultivate Cultural Contributions

Everyone in the expanding global economy faces the challenge of judging people fairly and on their individual performances regardless of cultural background. Unless performance is judged fairly, mutually rewarding relationships cannot exist. The best place to learn this vital human lesson is in the workplace. The more opportunities you receive to work closely with those from other cultures, the greater your personal growth can be.

Since most prejudice comes from fear of the unknown, those who attempt to understand another person's way of life will be less prejudiced and less likely to stereotype.

The work environment within a company, unit, department, or even a small team can be strengthened with people of diverse cultures working together. When several individuals from culturally diverse backgrounds contribute to a work team, the result can produce a wide range of ideas. Ideas provided by such a work team can help departments find creative solutions and alternatives to problems that a more homogeneous team might not discover. Since most companies are entering into, or at least are concerned about, international markets, the more diverse approach to problem solving also makes good business sense.

> *Avoid a stereotyped attitude:*
> *Walk a mile in the other*
> *person's shoes.*

# Case 13

**"Everybody has a problem these days."**

# Communication

Jack, a United States-born, European-educated biochemist, was disturbed emotionally after a late afternoon meeting. Why? Because it was just announced that Yoshio had received the appointment as manager of their bio-tech research team. It wasn't that Yoshio had not earned the promotion through his contribution to the team. Everyone recognized his skills. Besides, Yoshio also had seniority. Jack's negative reaction was based upon the premise that Yoshio was not a good communicator, and everyone on the team would suffer because of it. In Jack's opinion, Yoshio had not fully adapted to American ways. At times he was insensitive to the needs of co-workers. He was also a poor speaker in front of a group, and his leadership style was over-permissive.

Fortunately for Jack, he had recently received an offer from a competitive firm at a high salary with a more comprehensive benefit package. He could make the move at any time. The problem in accepting the new job was that it would necessitate a geographical move, which would make his wife and children unhappy. His wife is a medical doctor who is happy with her assignment at a fine local hospital. His two daughters are in high school and doing well with many friends. It would be unwise to disrupt such a good educational environment.

How should Jack view his choices? Is he upset emotionally because of some hidden prejudice? If Jack made the effort, could he build a mutually rewarding relationship with Yoshio, one that would give both parties a better future? Assume you are Jack's best friend and he comes to you for advice. How might you counsel Jack so that he would make the right decision for himself? (For a suggested answer, see page 230.)

# PART IV

# Building Your Career

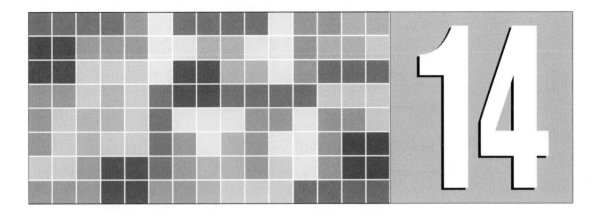

# Succeeding in a New Job or Assignment

**"There's more here than meets the eye."**

Thought for the Day: A good reason for giving your best effort in everything you do is to enjoy the many benefits of "effort ownership."

Undoubtedly you want to succeed on any new job or assignment you undertake. First, you want to prove to your family, friends, and management that you are a winner. Second, you want to prove it to yourself. Undoubtedly, there is a lot at stake when starting a new endeavor.

This chapter is devoted to ten tips that can help you in reaching your goal. If you take these tips seriously and apply them conscientiously, you can avoid many of the mistakes others make.

## Tip 1: Balance Home and Career

When you accept a new work challenge, it is vital that all home demands be under complete control. Your on-the-job concentration needs to be at a high level, and any home worries, especially those connected with small children or other relatives, can be distracting to both you and your co-workers. Balancing home and career, so that you can be a winner in both areas, is never easy to accomplish and maintain. The time to start (or reorganize) is *before* you accept a new job or assignment. Once things are out of balance, it may be too late for you to reach your full job potential. Give your career a break and get things organized at home *first*.

When it is necessary to call in ill, make every effort to talk with your supervisor or another management person. If a co-worker tells your boss you won't be in, doubts may be raised and your supervisor could call you for verification. Also, it never hurts to bring in a doctor's statement to document an extended absence.

## Tip 2: Use a Calendar Notebook to Help You Get Organized

An abundance of important information—rules, regulations, and procedures—will be thrown at you at the beginning of a new job. The first days are days of adjustment and excitement, so don't trust yourself to remember everything. Rather, buy an inexpensive calendar notebook or day-to-day organizer and use it to record some of the instructions and hard-to-remember information you get from your supervisor or fellow workers. Jot these data down as they are given to you.

Do not hesitate to take notes when receiving a complex answer to a question involving considerable detail. The notebook itself (if not overused) will create a good impression. It will help show that you are organized, methodical in your approach to learning, and serious about your career. In the evening, use the notebook to review certain facts and procedures. You can also use it to record appointments, ideas, names, and so on.

## Tip 3: Ask Questions, but Learn to Ask the Right Ones

Fear of being considered inadequate is the reason most people in a new work situation do not ask more questions. A genuine concern about making mistakes in a new position is understandable, but it is better to ask questions than to suffer the serious results of continued mistakes. If you don't understand something, ask questions until you do. Asking questions may be necessary because those responsible for your adjustment and training do not always take enough time to explain things fully. Because old hands tend to forget that they, too, had trouble learning at the beginning, they often talk so fast that only a genius or a psychic could get the message the first time around.

There is a right time and a wrong time to ask a question. One should not, for example, interrupt a person who is concentrating on getting a job done or who is communicating with others. There are also right and wrong questions. A right question is one you need to ask to be effective; a wrong question is one that does not apply to the task being explained. One should not, for example, ask questions that are answered in the orientation literature you have been given to read on your own time.

In asking questions, keep in mind that you must listen to the answers with your eyes as well as your ears. Sure, you receive the auditory impressions with your ears. But you should also look at the person who is speaking. Most people, in fact, feel it is discourteous when someone they are talking to lets his (or her) eyes wander. You will understand the importance of attentiveness if you have ever seen someone look at his watch, shuffle papers, stare at the floor, or look out a window while you are talking to him. You will make a better impression on people if you form the habit of listening with your eyes as well as your ears. You also stand a better chance of receiving any hidden—but vital—meaning that may lie under the message.

## Tip 4: Use Good Judgment in Working Extra Hours and Taking Your Breaks

Some employees with a new opportunity attempt to secure their jobs and attract management's attention by working more than the normal number of hours at the beginning. They arrive first in the morning and make a point of leaving last at the end of the day. They often skip their breaks. A zealous work attitude, if sincere, is to be admired.

However, overzealousness can get you into trouble on two counts. First, there are usually regulations governing hours to be worked. On certain jobs, unauthorized overtime work and failure to take breaks can involve you and your employer in labor difficulties. It is important, therefore, always to abide by the instructions given to you by management.

Second, your fellow employees may misinterpret your motives and make life more difficult for you and your supervisor. Working extra hours and eliminating breaks when an important deadline must be met and when you are asked to do it by your supervisor is one thing. Working extra hours only to impress others is quite another.

*As a rule, it is better to make full use of the time you spend on the job, rather than to try to impress others with your willingness to work extra hours.*

Many employees, especially those who are closely monitored by management, feel they need to immerse themselves in work as soon as they enter the workplace. It is often better to circulate around and send out a few friendly signals before digging into a day's work. Some people call this "doing a figure 8."

## Tip 5: Don't Flaunt Your Education or Previous Experience

You may have had more formal education than many of the people you will work with on your new job. But these people probably have far more on-the-job experience and practical know-how than you do. That being the case, you would be wise to let them discover your educational background and experience gradually.

The job you are assigned may be more difficult than you expect. If you try to impress people with your experience or intelligence, they may not want to give you any help when you most need it.

If you are an experienced employee, you may have received your job training in another company. You will probably find that things are done differently in your new firm. Perhaps your way of doing things is better. But until you are sure, be safe and do it the way people at your new job do it. Give your co-workers the satisfaction of explaining how they do things. You will have plenty of time later to make changes that can result in improvement for your work environment, products, or services.

It is also a good idea to keep your salary to yourself. It is possible that another employee, doing work similar to yours as you start out, has yet to reach your salary level. Misinterpretation and resentment might occur. If so, both you and the other employee could lose.

## Tip 6: Make Friends, but Don't Make Close Friends Too Soon

There are many little human-relations traps you can easily fall into in a new work environment. One of these is building one or two very strong friendships at the expense of all others. For example, suppose you discover that one of the employees in your department is extremely friendly the first day. Such friendliness is usually more than welcome the first few hours in a strange setting.

But beware. What if you spend all your time with this one employee and neglect being friendly to the others? What if this friendly person is not respected by the others? What if he (or she) has earned a poor reputation in the department and is offering you friendship from purely selfish motives?

Sometimes people who have failed to earn respect from others at work try desperately to win the friendship of a new employee. Remember that it is only natural that the other employees (including management) will quickly identify you with any employee or employees with whom you spend excessive time.

If one employee clings to you as you start your new job, you obviously have a difficult situation to handle. Of course, you should not be rude to this person. You will do well, however, to back away and be somewhat reserved toward this individual for the first few weeks and concentrate on building relationships with everyone.

## Tip 7: Look Energetic, but Don't Be an Eager Beaver

Some people start their careers with a great burst of energy and enthusiasm that cannot possibly be sustained. These people frequently create a favorable impression to begin with, but later on are reclassified by both management and their fellow workers.

It is easy to be overeager at the beginning. You are new to your job, so you have a fresh and dynamic approach. You have a lot of nervous energy to release. You are interested, and your interest motivates you to achieve. Your desire to succeed, however, might cause you to reach too far too fast.

The best way to make progress inside an organization is to make steady progress.

Goal setting is a good idea and may help you achieve an even work tempo. Daily goals, written down and accomplished according to a priority system, make you a more productive and valuable member of the team. The practice will also help you in preparing for a supervisory role.

## Tip 8: Different Organizations Have Different Personal Appearance and Grooming Standards

A few organizations, like factories, have no personal appearance or grooming standards. They are interested primarily in your work performance and your human-relations ability.

Other companies, especially those that do business directly with customers, set minimum standards that are usually easily met by most employees. Still other companies, like department stores, have rather high personal and grooming standards that may be difficult for some people to accept.

When you join an organization, carefully assess its standards and decide what is best for you and your future. You have a right to be yourself and protect your individuality. In doing so, however, you should weigh all factors and take into consideration that most people, including management, feel that a little conformity won't hurt you. You are responsible for meeting minimum dress standards. Managers quickly tire of those who try to slip by with unacceptable attire. They often interpret such behavior as immature.

## Tip 9: Read Your Employee Handbook and Other Materials Carefully

Many organizations publish handbooks and other materials for their employees. These pamphlets usually contain vital information. Yet many employees, especially those with experience elsewhere, never read them.

Don't be casual in your use of company literature. Where else can you learn company policies that can keep you out of trouble? Where else can you discover important data that will prevent you from asking unnecessary questions? Take home all of the literature you are given and devote some time to it. Understanding your company and the benefits provided will not only help you start on the right foot, it will further your career.

## Tip 10: Send Out Positive Verbal and Nonverbal Signals

There are many verbal signals you can use to create a good first impression. "Good morning" and "Thank you" are examples. Such easy signals of friendship should be transmitted with sincerity at every opportunity to acknowledge the presence of others and to recognize any courtesies they have extended to you, however small.

A friendly person—one who creates a good first impression—is also one who uses nonverbal signals. for example, a person with a ready smile is easily interpreted as a friendly person. The smile seems to break any psychological barriers that might exist in a meeting of strangers. You immediately feel adopted by the person who smiles. A smile, then, is a friendly, nonverbal signal.

There are many effective nonverbal signals in addition to the smile. Shaking hands, gesturing positively with the hand or head, opening doors for people—these are all signals you send that make it easier for people to meet and know you. When you send out such signals naturally and in good taste, others do not feel awkward about approaching you. You have made it easy for them, and they like you for it.

In communicating a positive attitude to co-workers or clients, body language is most important. You probably have heard people say, "That's no problem," while their attitude (communicated through their body language) demonstrated that it, indeed, was a problem.

People who develop confidence in sending out such signals of friendship make excellent first impressions. They quickly increase their sphere of influence and build many lasting working and personal relationships. Have confidence in yourself and your ability to send out such signals. Take the initiative. Send out your own brand of signals in your own style, and be a comfortable person to meet.

Remember, too, that the better you become at sending out sincere signals of friendship, the better prepared you will be for any job interviews you may face in the future.

> *Success can depend on luck; and to increase your propensity for luck, seek out opportunities and work hard.*

# Case 14

**"Whom can you trust?"**

# Nonprofessional

Thomas is the webmaster for a division of a company that is a major distributor of electronic components. Thomas is normally an honest individual. He would never think of taking office supplies for home use, for example, but he seems to feel that ideas are fair game. In practice, Thomas believes he is creative and resourceful. Thus, he thinks nothing of embellishing an idea created and introduced in casual conversation by a co-worker or another division webmaster and submitting it to his superior as if it were his own. Thomas is extremely good at e-mailing ideas to his boss. While many of his written suggestions are ideas discussed informally with other webmasters and co-workers in the organization, Thomas is not very good at giving others credit for their ideas.

Two weeks ago, Helen, one of Thomas's counterparts in another division, shared a layout idea at an informal luncheon meeting where Thomas was present. Yesterday morning, after a discussion with their common supervisor, Helen discovered that Thomas had submitted her layout idea as his. As a result, Thomas will receive a commendation at this Friday's staff meeting.

If you were Helen, what would you do? Where does ethics (or ethical behavior) fit into the practice of human relations at work? How is Thomas hurting himself by stealing other people's ideas? (For a suggested answer, see page 230.)

# Initiation Rites—Coping with Teasing and Testing

**"Seniority counts for something."**

Thought for the Day: No one understands better than you when you successfully negotiate one of life's difficult hurdles.

Getting started in a new job or assignment, where the setting is strange and the employees are strangers, is bound to give you a few psychological challenges. Rather than magnify these challenges, this chapter will help you understand why such problems sometimes develop—and, even more importantly, show you how you can handle them.

## Acceptance in Your New Environment

You may be assigned to a department as a replacement for someone the others hated to lose. They will need time to get used to you. You may not have the experience of the person you replaced, and as a result, others may have to work harder for a few days to get you started. It is even possible that someone in your new department wanted another person to have your job, and, as a result, there may be some resentment toward you.

It is never easy to be the newest member of a group. You cannot expect to go from being an outsider to being an insider without making a few adjustments. In the first place, you and your personality were forced upon the group. Probably they were not asked whether they wanted you. You have been, in effect, imposed upon them. Because they were there first, and because they probably have strong relationships among themselves, they may feel that you should earn your way into their confidence. It may not seem fair, but it is only natural for them to look at your arrival in a somewhat negative way.

Did you ever go through an initiation into a club? If so, you will understand that teasing or testing the new member is often a tradition. To a limited extent, the same can be true when a new employee joins a department or division in a business organization. There is nothing planned or formal about it, of course, but you should be prepared for a little good-natured teasing or testing. Let us look at the psychological reasons behind these two phenomena.

## Teasing

The teasing of a new employee is often nothing more than a way of helping the person become a full-fledged member of the group. It is a form of initiation rite that will help you feel you belong. Sometimes it is a group effort in which everyone participates. More often, however, it is an individual matter. *Teasing, for the most part, is harmless.*

The shop foreman who never had the advantage of a college education, but who has learned considerably from practical experience, might enjoy teasing a recent graduate of an engineering school. If the graduate engineer goes along with the teasing, a sound relationship between the two should develop. If, however, she (or he) permits it to get under her skin, the relationship could become strained.

The shop foreman's motive might be nothing more than a desire to help the new engineer build good relationships with the rest of the gang. There may be nothing resentful or personal about it.

A small group of employees who work together closely in a branch bank, lawyer's office, or other work-team environment can usually be expected to come up with a little harmless teasing when a new person joins the staff. He (or she) might be given the oldest equipment with a touch of formal ceremony or the dismal job of keeping the stockroom in order.

Usually, good-natured teasing is based upon tradition and human nature. People who like to tease in a harmless manner are generally good-natured. They enjoy people. They mean no harm. In fact, they usually do it to make you feel more, not less, comfortable.

If you are on the receiving end of some good, healthy teasing, you have nothing to worry about so long as you don't take it personally. Just go along with it and you'll come out ahead. It is much better to be teased than to be ignored. If by chance the baiting should go a little too far and you find yourself embarrassed, the very fact that it is embarrassing to you will probably make you some friends. A little good natured teasing that is handled well by you will help you get off to a good start on your new job. It will also help break down any communications barriers that might exist.

## Testing

Testing is different. It can have more serious implications. And testing will take more understanding on your part.

There are two kinds of testing. One is *organizational testing*. Organizational testing comes from the organization (management, personnel, or your supervisor) and is a deliberate attempt to discover what kind of person you really are and whether you can adjust to certain conditions. The other kind of testing—*personal testing*—comes strictly from individuals. Personal testing is one person trying out another because of personality conflicts or inner prejudices.

## Organizational Testing

Almost all kinds of organizations—especially the smaller ones—have certain unpleasant tasks that must be done. Frequently, these tasks are handed to the newest employee. The new salesperson in a department store may be given excessive amounts of stock work at the start of her (or his) career. The factory worker may be given unpleasant cleanup jobs until another new member joins the department. The clerical employee may be given a dreaded filing assignment as a way to get totally acquainted with the new position.

The important thing to recognize is that these tests have a purpose. Can the new worker take the assignment without complaining? Can he (or she) survive without developing a negative attitude? Will he accept the assignment as a challenge or show resentment and thereby destroy his chance of gaining the respect of the other members of the department?

The old phrase "starting at the bottom of the ladder" sometimes means exactly that. Many top management people started at the bottom, and they feel that "starting at the bottom" is the best way for you to start, too. If you can't take the mundane or "grunt" work at the onset of a new assignment, you may not be able to assume heavier responsibility later. It is the price you pay for being a beginner.

Management sometimes feels that "starting at the bottom" is the best way for the manager of the future to appreciate fully the kind of work that must be done by the entry-level employee. Many college graduates find themselves beginning their careers by doing the most uninviting tasks the company needs to have done. If they are human-relations smart, they will take it in stride, using the time to size up the situation and learn as much as possible about the organization.

During testing periods you are being watched by management and by your fellow employees. *The better you react, the sooner the testing will end and the better your relations with others will be.* In other words, although getting the job done is important, your attitude toward it may be more important. If you react in a negative manner, three things can happen:

- you may be kept on the assignment longer than you otherwise would have been,

- you may hurt your chances of getting a better assignment later on, and

- you may damage relationships with people involved in or observing the testing.

If you can take the long-range perspective and condition yourself to these tasks with an inner smile and an outward grin, you'll do well for yourself. Roll up your sleeves and get the job done quickly. If you finish one job, move on to another. Don't be afraid to get dirty. If you must take a little abuse, don't complain. It is part of the initiation rite, and someday you will look back on the experience as those ahead of you look back on it now. It would be foolhardy for the new employee to fight any of the many forms of organizational testing, as long as it doesn't seriously damage her (or his) personal dignity.

## Personal Testing

Personal testing is a different matter. It could give you more trouble, especially if you fail to recognize it for what it is. It may come from someone your own age or someone much older or younger. It may come from a fellow worker or from someone in management. You might be wise to start out with the attitude that everything is teasing rather than testing. Then, if it doesn't last long, you have automatically solved the problem.

But if the teasing continues for a long period of time, you will know that it is personal testing and that it is probably the product of a prejudice or genuine hostility. When this happens, you have a real challenge ahead of you. For example, one of your fellow employees may refuse to accept you. She (or he) may harass you at every turn and may not give you a chance to be a normal, productive employee. The needle will be out at every opportunity.

■ Example: Serious Testing #1

**Rayleen.**   When Rayleen was assigned to a maintenance crew with a gas and water company, she knew she was on a very strict 90-day probation period. The job was extremely important to her especially since it had taken her a long time to get it. She decided she would go all out to keep her personal productivity high and still build good relationships with the rest of the crew.

Everything would have been great if it had not been for Art. Art started out the very first day using every technique in the book to slow Rayleen down and get under her skin. Art constantly came up with comments like "What are you trying to do, Rayleen, make us all look bad?" "Who are you trying to impress by working so hard?" "If you slow down a little, we'll get you through probation."

After three weeks of heckling from Art, Rayleen knew she was up against a personality conflict loaded with hostility. Rather than take it any longer, she asked Art to meet her at a coffee shop after work. It was a strained evening, but Art finally relaxed. Much of the hostility disappeared, and the next day he was off Rayleen's back. Rayleen never knew for sure the real cause of the conflict. However, the crew seemed happier, and productivity was better.

Chances are good that personal testing will never happen to you personally; but, occasionally an employee will get on the receiving end of some nonorganizational or personal testing from a supervisor. Consider what happened to Romero in his first job.

■ Example: Serious Testing #2

**Romero.**   Romero graduated near the top of his class in nursing school. He took the first job he interviewed for as a vocational nurse in a community nursing home for elderly people. But Romero quickly discovered that he was on the receiving end of some rather vicious testing from his supervisor.

Romero was not surprised when he was assigned mostly extremely unpleasant tasks his first few days on the job. He knew it was traditional, so he pleasantly went about giving baths to some of the most difficult patients. He had many disagreeable duties, all of which were assigned to him by the supervisor. His supervisor was a registered nurse who had been at the home for many years.

Romero didn't complain; he didn't want any special favors. He took everything that came his way because he wanted to prove to himself that he could take it. But slowly he began to sense that something more than routine testing was involved. His supervisor seemed to dish out the ugly assignments with a strange, subtle bitterness. Not only that, but even after two new vocational nurses had joined the staff, Romero was still doing all the really dirty jobs.

Although he was fearful of prejudice from the beginning, he tried to play it cool and hoped for a change. He said nothing. But soon his fellow workers, most of whom were his age and also vocational nurses, got the message. When they did, a confrontation took place that finally reached the desk of the nursing home owner. The pressure on Romero was quickly removed. No one was sorry a week later when the registered nurse responsible for the problems resigned.

It is sometimes impossible to know the deep-seated motives behind some of the serious testing that takes place. Often the people responsible do not know themselves. Prejudice—whether it be associated with age, race, sex, jealousy, or other factors—is only one of the many causes. Consider the case involving Mario.

■ Example: Serious Testing #3

**Mario.**    Mario was really pleased about his new construction job. At last he would be able to put his apprenticeship training to work and make some good money. He anticipated all the teasing he got from the old-timers at the beginning, and he took it in stride without any big scenes. But his foreman's attitude was something else. No matter how hard he tried, Mario got the needle from his foreman at every turn. No matter how much work Mario turned out, the foreman was on his back. Mario took it for about a week, and then, in desperation, he asked the advice of one of the older crew members. Here is what the older man said: "Look, buddy, our beloved supervisor is an uptight conservative. Your long hair, your flashy sports car, and especially your free and easy lifestyle all get to him. Frankly, I think he has some trouble with his own sons, and you remind him of them. At any rate, he's all wrong. What you do to get him off your back, though, is your own problem. Good luck."

Mario gave it some serious thought and decided that he would face the foreman and see what happened. It was a tough decision to make because he didn't want to lose his job. He waited until they were alone, and then he put all his cards on the table. He said, "You've been on my back, and you know it. I think you should either tell me why or start treating me the way you treat the others." There were some tense and awkward moments. But when it was all over, the foreman managed a small smile. From then on, things were noticeably better for Mario.

These three examples represent only a few of the many different cases that could be presented.

# Addressing Negative Testing

Sometimes testing can present a challenge for you in your new job. Sometimes supervisors are responsible; sometimes they are not. The question is, of course, what can you do if you come up against a serious testing situation?

Here are a few pointers that may help you.

Accept the testing situation willingly until you have time to analyze it carefully. Take testing as part of the initiation period and conduct yourself in such a manner as not to aggravate the situation. It may pass by itself, or someone else, without your knowledge, may come to your rescue. If time does not take care of it and you come to the point where you sincerely feel that you are being pushed too far, approach the person who is doing the needling with a "let's lay all the cards on the table" attitude. In your own words, without hostility, say something like this: "If I have done anything to upset you, please tell me. Otherwise, I feel it is time we started to respect each other."

Confronting the negative situation will not be easy for you to do. But in cases of extreme testing, it is necessary to make the tester account for his (or her) actions. There is no other solution.

Unfortunately, some individuals will push you around indefinitely if you permit it. And if you permit it, they will never respect you. Chances are that you will not be subjected to excessive pushiness by your supervisor. But if you are, you must stand up to the situation and solve it yourself. It is important to you and to the company that you do so.

Of course, you need to go about addressing negative testing in the right way. Try not to have a chip on your shoulder. Do not make accusations. Try not to say anything personal about the person needling you. Your goal is to open up the relationship, to find a foundation upon which you can build for the future. Your goal is to demolish the psychological barrier, not to find out who is responsible for it. You must make it easy for the other person to save face.

In most cases of testing (even when a healthy relationship has yet to be built), the principles and techniques found in Chapter 12 are applicable, and it may be helpful for you to consider them.

Unless the testing is extremely severe or prolonged, you may be better off not going to others either inside or outside your organization for help. You will be respected for taking care of the problem yourself. If, however, you have made every effort to clear up the problem over a reasonable length of time and you have had no success, you should go to your supervisor and discuss it honestly and freely. Situations of this kind should not be permitted to continue to the point where departmental morale and productivity are impaired.

If you can prove that discrimination or sexual harassment has been involved, you should feel free to take your case to your company's affirmative action officer or to your local Equal Employment Opportunity Commission.

It is important not to anticipate encountering negative and excessive testing and teasing in your new job. If you do anticipate it, however, you are sure to "find" what you are looking for and end up making more out of the situation than you would have if you had been more positive. By keeping a positive outlook, you may never encounter the rare occasion when such a problem may come your way. You may even get through a rather negative situation without even realizing it, mainly because you took a positive approach to handle it. For the most part, teasing and testing will be good-natured—maybe even enjoyable—if you have the right attitude.

> *If you can turn a negative situation into a positive one, you have conquered one of the most powerful attributes known to man.*

# Case 15

**"A person's attitude can stand just so much."**

# Confrontation

John graduated from a state college as a consumer science major. He was ambitious, talented, and determined. In practically no time at all he had found a good position with a highly reputable retail operation. His position involved working in a laboratory where all consumer products purchased by the buyers were tested for safety, wearability, and other standards.

John received many compliments on his work from his supervisor. In addition, he was able to build good relationships with all his co-workers except Ms. Robertson. Ms. Robertson was a long-time employee and very critical of John. She constantly made unkind and seemingly uncalled for remarks about John.

John decided it was time to do something about the growing negative relationship with Ms. Robertson. By checking around, John discovered that two previous employees had resigned because of Ms. Robertson. Feeling a little better that there was probably nothing personal about the trouble he was having, John waited for the right opportunity to meet with Ms. Robertson. This is what John said to her:

"Ms. Robertson, I have been here for two months and I seem to be getting along with everyone but you. I like my job. I want to keep it. If I have done anything to offend you, please tell me and I'll certainly make a change. I want very much to win your respect, but I do not intend to put up with your unfair treatment of me any longer."

Did John do the right thing? Was he too forceful in his approach? What would you have done in his place? If you were the supervisor, how would you resolve the conflict? (For a suggested answer, see page 230).

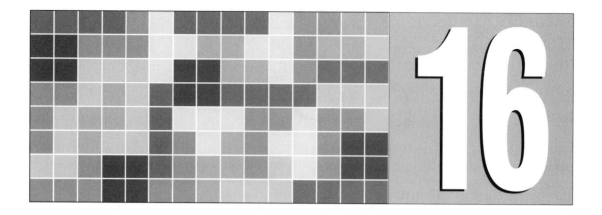

# Absenteeism and
# Human Relations

**"What? Late again?"**

Thought for the Day: Even the very best intentions can never take the place of being dependable, punctual, reliable, and credible.

"Sorry I didn't show up for work yesterday, Rich. I had a little too much to drink at Harry's party, so I decided to stay in the sack and sleep it off."

"Hope things weren't too hard on you last Friday, Alice. I had a case of the blahs, so I stayed home and got a few personal things taken care of."

"Did you hear that sick crack from my supervisor, Marge? She surely gets up-tight when I'm a little late now and then. You'd think that I'd committed a major crime."

"Don't breathe a word to the boss, Linda, but I'm going to make this a three-day weekend so I can go on a hiking trip. See you Tuesday."

"I've got to sneak out and take care of something personal, Bob. Cover for me while I'm gone, will you?"

Absenteeism is a phenomenon that management lives with on a daily basis. So are the problems of lateness and of employees leaving their work stations without authorization. Most experts agree that fewer and fewer people are taking pride in their attendance or on-time records. Why?

Those close to the scene have come up with many answers why work absenteeism is increasing. Here are four reasons that are frequently cited: (1) people do not commit themselves to a career or company as much these days (partially because organizations no longer value loyalty as much as they did in the past), so employees do not feel as much pressure to live up to the rules; (2) schools and colleges are so relaxed that the adjustment to the discipline of business is more difficult than it was in the past; (3) many people no longer feel obligated to live up to attendance standards or rules imposed on them by organizations; and (4) people allow personal problems to spill over into their work environment more than in the past.

## Absenteeism Policy

What is the basic policy that most business and government organizations have toward absenteeism and reporting to work late? What is acceptable and what is not? What is management's attitude toward the problem, and what action does it take with those who consistently violate their policies?

Most professional managers in business and government endorse and try to get their employees to live within the framework and spirit of the following policy:

Employees should not come to work when one of the following conditions exist:

1. when it might endanger their own health or that of their co-workers;

2. when the employee is in a psychological or emotional state that could hurt on-the-job productivity and possibly create an unsafe condition; or

3. when a serious personal or family emergency exists.

*If none of the above conditions exists, employees should be on the job and, except in special cases, they should be there on time.*

This basic absenteeism policy might sound harsh and autocratic, but organizations have had years of experience with the problem; and they feel that unless they take a firm stand, they will be misinterpreted by some and taken advantage of by others.

## Need for a Policy

In order to make a profit and stay in business, most organizations must operate under tight production and service schedules. These schedules are built around employees. An assembly line from which a few workers are absent is no longer an assembly line. When a customer wants to buy something in a retail store and there is no one available to help, a sale can be lost. A customer goes to a restaurant and if the waitperson is doing the work of two because another waitperson didn't show up, the customer may never return.

Management has learned that when an employee or supervisor doesn't show up for work as scheduled, immediate and costly adjustments are necessary if production is to continue and customers are to be kept happy. Sometimes, but not always, the other employees can pitch in and fill the gap. But most of the time, the company pays at least a small price in loss of efficiency, loss of sales, or loss of customer faith. In short, the absence of an employee usually costs the company money in one way or another. If the absence is necessary, no one complains. But if the absence is unnecessary, then management must become concerned and involved.

Chronic lateness by an employee, although not usually as serious or expensive for the company as absenteeism, is still a problem. A late employee can delay the changing of shifts. An employee who is constantly late can upset a conscientious supervisor and make her (or him) more difficult for others to work with for the rest of the day. Most serious of all is the negative influence the consistently late employee has on the productivity of others. The supervisor who takes a soft approach to such an employee stands the chance of losing the respect of other, more reliable employees.

## Employee Challenges

But absenteeism, lateness, and unauthorized time away from work are not only management problems. They should also be viewed as problems and challenges to the employee. That is primarily what this chapter addresses. How should *you* look at these problems? How will they influence your future?

Supervisors and workers who fail to build a good record in these areas will almost always pay a very high price in terms of their relationships with others. Here is why.

■ *A poor attendance record will keep you from building good horizontal work-ing relationships with your co-workers. Your co-workers may deeply resent having to carry an extra load when you are absent.* Few kinds of behavior will destroy a relationship more quickly than being frequently absent and causing co-workers to "carry" you in your own department.

■ *A poor record will strain the vertical working relationship with your super-visor. It will make more work for her (or him) personally, it will cause her department to be less efficient, and it will put her on the spot with other em-ployees.* Most experts agree that it is almost impossible for an employee who is guilty of chronic absenteeism to maintain a healthy relationship with an immediate supervisor.

In addition to the preceding two basic reasons, the following four rea-sons should receive consideration.

1. Excessive absenteeism and lateness will build a credibility gap between you and management. A credibility gap can seriously hurt your future because those who cannot be depended upon are seldom promoted. It should also be pointed out that, right or wrong, some management people feel there is a moral aspect to the problem. If an individual ac-cepts employment, he (or she) agrees to abide by the rules, within rea-son. Absence without sufficient cause is interpreted by management as moral failure.

2. Records that reflect heavy absenteeism and lateness are permanent and can be forwarded upon request to other organizations. The record you are building now could help or hurt you should you decide to move elsewhere.

3. If you have a good record, a request to be absent for personal and non-emergency reasons will seem more acceptable.

4. In case of layoffs, cutbacks, and reassignments, those people with poor records are usually the first to be terminated or reassigned.

Most organizations want to be understanding about employees' prob-lems. They realize that there are exceptions to the rules, and they are will-ing to listen and make adjustments. Employees who consistently abuse the rules are usually counseled and given adequate warning. Those who play it straight with their companies usually receive fair and just treatment in re-turn. To illustrate the causes and results of absenteeism and lateness among employees and supervisors, the following five examples are cited.

**Dennis.** Dennis was a productive worker. When he was on the job and feeling well, nobody could complain about him. He had plenty of skill, a great sense of humor, and was always willing to pitch in and help others.

His only real problem was drinking. Every other week he would really tie one on and call in sick.

About a year ago, Dennis and his supervisor had a series of heart-to-heart talks about Dennis's drinking. Three months later, Dennis and a counselor from the human resource department discussed the problem on three different occasions. Six months ago—half a year since his first talk with the supervisor—Dennis was referred to the company physician for professional help. Last week, with full documentation by the organization, Dennis was reluctantly given his termination notice. His record showed that he had been absent more than thirty days the previous year. The organization Dennis worked for had tried to help, but Dennis had refused to help himself.

**Judy.** When she first came to work, Judy showed great promise. She had all the skills necessary to become a top-flight employee, and she was great with people. Among some of the staff, she quickly became known as the "too" girl. She was too pretty, too vivacious, and too popular. She also received too many invitations to too many parties, and as a result, she was absent too frequently.

It became clear to her supervisor that Judy just didn't have the physical endurance to lead such an active social life and hold down a demanding full-time job at the same time. During the first six months of employment she was absent eleven times, each time for one day, and her excuse was always illness. After repeated counseling, Judy's supervisor finally asked that she transferred to another department. Management made an attempt to transfer her, but when other supervisors checked on her absentee record, they refused to accept her. After additional unsuccessful counseling, management had to let her go.

**Katherine.** Katherine was highly ambitious, talented, energetic, and respected by both fellow employees and management. Everybody expected her to move a long way up the executive ladder. She seemed programmed for success. But Katherine's desire for quick recognition and more money caused her to hurt her reputation inside the company. Here is the story.

Katherine took a moonlighting job with a musical group that was good enough to get four or five bookings each week. The job paid good money, but it demanded a lot of energy. After a few months, Katherine not only looked beat, but her on-the-job productivity started to drop. Soon she started calling in sick from time to time. Within six months, she had seriously hurt her reputation.

Fortunately for Katherine, she had an understanding supervisor. After some counseling, Katherine quit her moonlighting and started to build back the fine reputation she had once enjoyed. It cost her at least one promotion, but Katherine did learn one lesson: any outside activity that drains one's energy to the point where frequent absences are necessary eventually spells trouble.

**Vinnie.** Vinnie was an excellent salesperson in a fashion department. He was so good, in fact, that he was being trained as a fashion coordinator and buyer. But Vinnie had one bad habit that he could not shake. He could not organize his day to the point where he could get to work on time. His timecard showed that he was five to fifteen minutes late two or three times each week.

Vinnie's supervisor and the store manager counseled him. Nobody wanted to lose him, but in the final analysis, management had to weigh the influence of his lateness on the morale and productivity of others. Reluctantly, the decision to release Vinnie was made. He didn't have any trouble getting another job, but the new job didn't have the potential of the one he had lost, and the new management was less tolerant of his problem.

**Gloria and Sammy.**   A national chain organization was forced to cut back its work force because of lower sales. It was decided that they could get by with one instead of two employees in a particular department in one of their stores. One individual, either Gloria or Sammy, would be transferred to a less desirable job in another section.

A careful analysis was made to see which of the two people should be moved. Both were highly respected, and they were equal in all but two respects. Gloria had three years' seniority over Sammy, so normally she would stay. But Gloria's absentee record was much poorer than Sammy's. Management decided that because Sammy had the better attendance record, he deserved to keep the better job. When Gloria was notified and given the reason for the decision, she admitted she had no defense even though she had seniority.

These cases are just a few examples of how employees can hurt their long-range careers by frequent absenteeism or chronic lateness.

# Attendance Record Tips

Here are a few tips that will help you be a conscientious employee who does not abuse the company policy on absenteeism and lateness.

1. Stay home under the following conditions: (a) when you are honestly sick and feel it would hurt your health or that of others if you reported to work, (b) when your emotional or mental condition is such that you know you could not contribute to the productivity of the department and might endanger the safety of others, and (c) when you have a family emergency and are urgently needed.

2. Notify the company at once of your decision to be away from work. Tell your supervisor in an honest and straightforward way why you can't make it. Talk to your supervisor, not to a co-worker.

3. If you stay at home for more than a single day because of illness, it is wise to provide a daily progress report on your condition. Also, estimate when you will be able to return.

4. Save your authorized sick-leave time for real emergencies. It is a cushion that might come in handy. If you never use it, you should assume the attitude that you were lucky you didn't have to do so.

5. Always give yourself a little lead time when getting ready to report to work. Do not put yourself in a position where a small delay will make you late. It is better to be ten minutes early than one minute late. On those rare occasions when you are late, give management a real reason for it.

6. Take your allotted breaks, but don't be absent from your work station longer than the specified time. People who always stretch their coffee breaks are not appreciated by their co-workers or supervisor. When emergencies do come up and you must forgo or delay a scheduled break, don't nurse the feeling that you have been cheated and that you need an extra-long break to make up for it.

7. Don't be absent from your work station for long, unless you work it out in advance with your supervisor. Also, let your co-workers and/or your supervisor know where you will be when you are away. The best way to keep a supervisor from breathing down your neck is to earn your freedom by keeping him (or her) adequately informed.

8. When you have a special reason for being absent from work, such as a family wedding, funeral, or court appearance, work it out with your supervisor as far in advance as possible.

9. In planning for a pregnancy leave or seeking a leave of absence to act as a care provider for a family member, work out the details with your superior or the department of human resources as far in advance as possible. Make appropriate plans for a competent temporary replacement to be located and trained, so that productivity levels will not suffer during your absence.

A good attendance record shows management that you are sensitive to the needs of others. It shows them that you are a motivated rather than a reluctant worker. It shows them that you are ready for better opportunities.

> *Continual excuses for work*
> *missed may permanently excuse*
> *a person from work.*

# Case 16

**"Nobody could balance my act."**

# Balance

Lorraine works in the Internal Documents unit of a large gas and oil firm. She is an assistant to Mr. Hodges whose job it is to write employee manuals relating to company policies and procedures. Lorraine assists Mr. Hodges in updating the company database and informing all the right people in the company as soon as a manual is in effect and available to them.

It is easy to like Lorraine. She is highly efficient at her job, always will-ing to pitch in to help others, and often forgoes her break or stays late to catch up on her work. There is only one major problem that Lorraine has that creates real concern for her supervisor and co-workers: excessive absen-teeism. Some of Lorraine's co-workers often bet on just which day of the week she will fail to show up.

The problem lies in Lorraine's inability to balance home and career. A single parent (a highly protective mother of a three-year-old daughter, Sissy), Lorraine sometimes stays home to catch up on home chores, to change babysitters, or when Sissy has the sniffles. When Lorraine calls in (she doesn't always phone), her excuse almost always relates to an illness—either her own or Sissy's.

Over the last three months, departmental productivity has dropped measurably because of adjustments made to compensate for Lorraine's ab-sences. For example, Lorraine's co-workers are frequently pulled away from their work to do hers. Reassigned employees must be informed in a timely manner about company mergers and on-going sensitive acquisitions. Infor-mation must be conveyed at proper times and coordinated with employee transfers, lay-offs, and other critical events that, if delayed, could create se-rious legal implications for the company. Mr. Hodges needs someone who he can depend on to meet deadlines and who takes responsibility for job assignments. Lorraine's work is commendable, but Mr. Hodges never knows when he can count on her to get it done (or when he has to follow up and reassign her work).

All in all, Lorraine's relationships with Mr. Hodges and co-workers are paper thin.

How far, in your opinion, should Lorraine's supervisor and company go to protect Lorraine's job? (For a suggested answer, see page 231.)

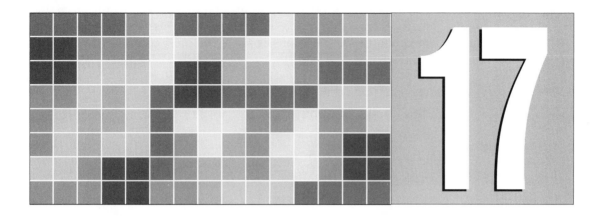

# Six Common Human-Relations Mistakes

**"Mistakes? Don't look at me!"**

Thought for the Day: It is totally unrealistic to expect a quality result without giving a quality effort.

Both new and experienced employees make human-relations mistakes that damage their personal progress. It is the purpose of this chapter to single out and fully explain the implications of six of the most common mistakes:

1. Failure to listen

2. Underestimating others

3. Failure to report or admit mistakes to management

4. Failure to provide your own motivation

5. Permitting others to turn you into a victim

6. Falling prey to negative drift

## Failure to Listen

The art of listening is a basic human-relations skill. Many excellent books on the subject can be found in your public library and local book stores. If you read just one, you will improve your competency in this area. Our discussion of the art of listening will be brief and to the point.

Listening requires concentration. *Thus, the first step in learning how to listen is to learn how to concentrate.* Hearing is a selective process. Most people hear only what they want to hear. Your problem, then, is to listen to what is important and push other sounds to the outer edge of your hearing. There are so many sounds around you that you may not be picking up the ones that are vital to your happiness and success.

On the job, hearing is a matter of practical communication. When a supervisor or fellow worker wishes to transmit an idea, a warning, or a change in procedure to you, he (or she) frequently does it verbally. There may be other sounds he cannot eliminate. It may be the end of the day, and you may be tired. His words may mean one thing to him and another to you. Good, clear, accurate communication is never easy.

Let us assume, however, that the person initiating the message does the best job possible. Does this ensure that you will receive the message? Of course not! You are the receiver, and if your mind is focused elsewhere when the message is transmitted, *you may hear the sounds but fail to get the message.*

Advertising executives and specialists have recognized for years how difficult it is to get a verbal message home. The difficulty is most apparent in television commercials. There, the name of the product is often repeated six or more times in thirty seconds. If you are really listening, you might feel that such repetition is an insult to your ability to receive. You would be justified in having this reaction. But the advertising people do not assume that you are a good listener. They assume that you are a typical (that is, poor) listener. Consequently, to be sure the product name makes an impression, they pound it home through repetition.

Your supervisor is not an advertising expert, nor does she (or he) have the time to pound her message home. She feels she should be able to say it once and have it understood. She assumes you are a good listener.

Sometimes it is very difficult just to sit back and listen. There are three basic reasons why listening is difficult:

- People are often so busy with their own thoughts and desires, related and nonrelated, they are 90 percent sender and only 10 percent receiver. When this happens, the communication system breaks down.

- Some individuals are so self-centered they think only in terms of themselves. That is, instead of listening to what is being said, they merely wait for the speaker to finish so they can talk. Getting their thoughts organized keeps them from being good listeners.

- Some people allow themselves to analyze the motives or personality traits of the person speaking and, again, fail to hear what is being said.

In business and industry, the ability to listen is often a matter of dollars and cents. A draftsman who doesn't hear an architect tell him to make a certain change in a blueprint can cause the loss of thousands of dollars when a bid is accepted on specifications that are not correct. A salesperson who fails to hear a message from a client, and as a result does not comply with an important delivery date, can lose not only the sale but also a valued customer.

Communication problems can also cost money in factories. For example, Dan's failure to receive and retain the right message from his shop foreman cost his company a considerable amount of money. Here is the story.

> **Dan.** On his way to his regular morning coffee break, and somewhat pre-occupied with his own thoughts, Dan was stopped by his foreman and told to change the tolerance on a machine part he would be turning out for the rest of the day. After his coffee break, Dan returned to his machine, made an adjustment, and worked hard the rest of the day to complete all of the parts. The following day he was called on the carpet for producing parts that were too small. What had happened? Dan had been told to increase the size of the part, but he had decreased it instead. His failure to receive— and retain—the right message was a serious mistake, and it cost his company money in terms of both time and materials.

You can think of many other examples. It can even be said that when safety precautions are the subject of the message, the ability to listen can be a matter of life and death.

Let's look at your ability to listen from the viewpoint of your supervisor who is, after all, the primary sender of important messages to you. Here are some questions you can ask yourself to determine whether you are a good listener:

- Does your supervisor have to fight to get your attention?

- Do you find yourself thinking about something else the moment your supervisor starts talking?

- Does your supervisor insult you by repeating the message because she (or he) senses you are a poor listener? Or do you find you must go back and ask the supervisor to repeat it?

- Do you sometimes feel confused about instructions given to you when you start to do the requested job?

If you can say "no" to these questions, you may be a good listener. If not, you should concentrate on improving your listening skills. The following listening tips should help you.

## Tips for Listening

1. Always look at the person who is sending the message. Looking at the speaker will help you concentrate and close out unimportant noises. Your eye contact also will send a message to the speaker that you are listening.

2. If your supervisor has trouble sending out clear signals, you must make the extra effort to listen more carefully. Although it is primarily his (or her) responsibility to be a good sender, it is still to your advantage to receive the message as clearly as possible.

3. To remember the message, take some notes. Review the notes. Repeat the message in your mind a few times. Put any change ordered in the message into practice as soon as possible. When appropriate, repeat the message to your supervisor.

4. Refrain from coming up with an excuse when you receive criticism. You will improve more if you listen to what you are doing wrong rather than quickly coming to your own defense.

5. Think, reply briefly if necessary, and then continue to listen, so that you receive the complete message.

6. Always ask questions right away if you don't understand something. If you don't ask for clarification of a point, you may not fully get the message that follows.

7. If you find yourself in conversation with someone who is overly talkative, do not hesitate to interrupt after a polite period of time. If you do not interrupt, you may become so irritated you may not listen anyway.

Being a good listener is not easy. It will take a conscientious effort on your part. But one of the finest compliments you will ever receive from a superior will be something like this: "One thing I really like about Harry is that if you tell him something once, you know he's got it. You never have to tell him twice."

# Underestimating Others

The second of the six big mistakes, according to human resources people, is that of underestimating others.

A superior or co-worker may not appear to be doing much from your limited perspective. You might, therefore, wrongly assume that he (or she) is coasting. Assuming could be a big mistake.

Here is a simple case to emphasize the point.

**Henry.** Once Henry .completed the 30-day training program of his new job with a major metropolitan department store, he was assigned to Ms. Smith, the manager of inexpensive women's apparel.

Henry soon discovered that he was part of a rather hectic operation. Merchandise moved in and out of the department quickly. Ms. Smith was not an impressive person to Henry. Her desk was disorderly. She seemed to move in many directions at the same time. She seemed to spend more time than necessary talking to the employees.

Henry decided that he had drawn an unfortunate first assignment.

It was his good luck to meet a young buyer at lunch one day. From this woman he learned that Ms. Smith had the most profitable department in the store and an outstanding reputation with all top management people. Ms. Smith had trained more of the store's executives than any other person. It was then obvious that Henry had received one of the best assignments and had seriously underestimated Ms. Smith.

The new employee in this case learned an important lesson without getting hurt. He quickly changed his attitude toward his supervisor before the relationship was seriously damaged. He was fortunate.

When you fail to build a quality relationship with a supervisor or co-worker because you underestimate her (or him), you may hurt yourself in the following ways.

■ Your negative attitude may cause you to learn less from a supervisor or co-worker than you otherwise would.

■ Coworkers may sense the mistake you are making and see your attitude as a sign of immaturity.

■ The individual you have misjudged may sense your attitude and resent it, causing a serious human-relations problem.

If you are a new employee or have recently accepted a new assignment, remind yourself that you are in the poorest position to estimate the power, influence, and contribution that others are making to the organization, *especially when these people are already in management positions*. You will be smart to avoid prejudging others. Different people make different contributions to the growth and profit of an organization. Top management can see the whole picture, but usually you cannot as a new employee.

If the temptation is too great and you must at times question the effectiveness of others, keep your impressions to yourself. You can easily trap yourself by being a Monday morning quarterback. Underestimating the value of others can keep you from building relationships that are important to your personal progress.

## Failure to Report or Admit Mistakes to Management

A third common human-relations mistake is failure to admit or report to management personal errors in judgment or violations of company procedures, rules, and regulations.

Everyone makes minor blunders from time to time. Even a good employee is not perfect. Precise and methodical people sometimes make mistakes in calculations. Logical thinkers who pride themselves on their scientific approach to decision making sometimes make an error in judgment. A conscientious person who is very loyal to the organization will, on occasion, violate a company rule or regulation before he (or she) knows it.

These things happen to the best of people, and unless you are a most unusual person, they will happen to you. These little mistakes will not damage your career if you admit them openly. They can, however, cause considerable damage if you try to cover them up and, in so doing, compound the original mistake. To illustrate, let us take the incident of the dented fender.

> **Kari.**   One of Kari's numerous responsibilities working for a large bank was to deliver documents to various branch operations in the banking system. To make her deliveries, she checked out a company car from the transportation department.
>
> On one such assignment, Kari dented the fender of a company car while backing out of a crowded parking lot. She knew that she should report the damage to the dispatcher, but the dent was so insignificant that she thought it would go unnoticed. Why make a federal case out of a little scratch? Why spoil a clean record with the company over something so unimportant?
>
> Two days later, Kari was called into the private office of her department manager. It was an embarrassing twenty minutes. She had to admit that she was responsible for the damage and that she had broken a company rule by not reporting it. The incident was then closed.
>
> The slight damage to the company car was a human error anyone could make. The big mistake Kari made was in not reporting it. Looking back on the incident, she admitted that the damage to the car was far less than the damage to her relationships with others.

Most little mistakes, and sometimes many big mistakes, are accepted and forgotten when they are openly and quickly reported. Throwing up a smoke screen to cover them is asking for trouble. The second mistake may be more damaging than the first.

# Failure to Provide Your Own Motivation

The modern approach by management to provide the best possible working environment—and *then give employees the freedom to motivate themselves in their own way*—often leaves a few individuals on the sidelines unmotivated. It is a human-relations mistake to allow yourself to fall into this category.

New employees are expected to possess sufficient self-confidence to engage in the normal work process without always having to be nudged by others; experienced workers are expected to stay alert and productive without special counseling by their supervisors. Those who stand or sit around while co-workers are busily involved in productivity set themselves apart and, in so doing, injure their relationships with both supervisors and fellow employees.

In the workplace, everyone is expected to be a part of the team and contribute at acceptable levels. Those who wait around expecting or refusing to be motivated leave themselves on the sideline where learning opportunities and promotional possibilities are limited.

Of course, anyone can occasionally have an off day. But self-motivation is primarily an attitude of consistent willingness to do whatever it takes (within legal and ethical bounds) to get the job done while meeting established timeliness and quality standards. Initially, it may take some extra effort to get your internal (self-motivation) generator going. Be willing to try harder and go the extra mile for your organization without constant prodding. More than likely, your managers will be more willing to reciprocate. See Chapter 21 for more insight into self-motivation.

# Permitting Others to Turn You into a Victim

When people are unfortunate and become victims of automobile accidents or needless crimes, they often pay a high price. The consequences can be similarly serious when we become human-relations victims. Consider the following:

- Statistically, only a small percentage of people become direct victims of serious crime. Everyone eventually becomes a victim of a damaged relationship.

- Financial loss due to robbery, fraud, or physical injury can be high. So can the loss of a career opportunity that results from unrepaired relationships.

- The emotional and psychological damage of being a human-relations victim can sometimes be as traumatic as being a victim of crime. Becoming a victim of a damaged relationship can cause moodiness, loss of confidence, resentfulness, indignation, and mental distress.

There are three primary ways people needlessly victimize themselves:

1. when they refuse to correct human-relations mistakes quickly;

2. when they do not make an effort to correct a no-fault situation; and

3. when they permit the emotionalism of a relationship conflict to churn them up inside.

Many times a conflict will emerge within a relationship and both parties will become increasingly involved in a process that accelerates to more damaging stages.

*Stage 1:* There is only surface damage, low "hurt" involvement. Restoration possibilities are excellent. No harm done.

*Stage 2:* Emotional damage is usually more serious for one individual than the other. Restoration is more difficult.

*Stage 3:* As a result of lack of communication, conflict becomes needlessly severe. Both parties become victims. Professional counseling may be needed.

The victimization process will vary depending on the individuals and the nature of the conflict. Once started, however, it often becomes a continuous development, until both parties end up losers. Thus, the sooner any damage—no matter how slight—is repaired, the better. Just as both individuals can become victims, both can also become winners.

To help the reader avoid self-victimization, the following suggestions are made.

- Read Chapter 11 a second time to learn how to release your aggressions harmlessly.

- Remember that the more meaningful a relationship is to you, the higher the risk of self-victimization should a conflict occur.

- A substitute phrase for *self-victimization* is *holding a grudge.*

- Let small irritations pass.

- Every time a relationship conflict occurs, ask yourself this question: *Who will become the ultimate victim?*

Obviously as you become more competent at human relations, fewer conflicts will surface and there is less of a chance that you will become a victim. But once a conflict develops, you become vulnerable and the steps you take to restore the relationship are critical. If you are not willing to take action (regardless of who may be at fault), you may nullify much of the human-relations progress you have made.

# Falling Prey To Negative Drift

Frequently, there is a subtle but consistent pressure that pushes us from positive to negative thinking. For lack of a better term, let's call this phenomenon *negative drift*. Similar to a pall of dark smoke that hides a sunny landscape, negative drift is a gloomy cloud that prevents us from seeing the more positive factors in our lives.

What are the causes of negative drift? Most people believe negative drift occurs because there are increasingly more and more negative factors to contend with in today's society. For example,

- jobs are faster paced and more stressful;

- there is more crime, violence, traffic, litigation, and bureaucracy; and

- the media provides an overdose of negative images.

The premise, then, is that we all must live in an environment with more negative stimuli, and, if we are not cautious, we become more negative *without knowing that it is happening*.

So how can we avoid becoming prey to negative drift? Most people agree that a strong counterforce is necessary. The problem intensifies when we recognize that an opposing force must be sufficiently powerful to hold back negative drift. Negative drift can creep up on us without our knowing it, and, at the same time, cause us to lose focus on the positive factors in our jobs and personal lives. In other words, it is more of a challenge to stay positive in our society today than it was in the past.

Reflect for a moment and select the most consistently positive person you know. Now ask yourself this question: Does this individual have to work at it each day to stay positive? Chances are that the answer is a resounding "yes." Even when people have few negatives in their lives, they must continue to "prop up" their attitudes on a daily basis to keep negative drift from taking over.

> *If your attitude barometer suggests the need for a change in weather, give it a positive upturn.*

# Case 17

**"Barry's okay—he just needs motivation."**

# Motivation

Barry seemed to have everything going for him: He graduated with academic honors near the top of his class without putting in a lot of extra effort. He had acquired an excellent general knowledge and had mastered a wide range of technical skills well beyond the level of many of his classmates. Barry also had excellent human-relations skills, enjoyed sports, and was able to balance his many talents with exceptional ability.

With all of Barry's advantages, one would expect him to be highly successful in his first position as he starts his work career. Not so. For some reason, Barry doesn't even begin to live up to his potential. Could it be that as an only child he has accepted too much emotional and financial support from his family? Is Barry lazy? Is everything too easy for him? Is he too easygoing?

After six months on the job, Barry's boss called him into his office for a discussion. Barry's boss put it to him this way: "Barry, you truly do have everything going for you, but for some reason, you expect others to motivate you. Your inability to be a self-starter is putting you out of step with your co-workers. Frankly, I don't have the time or patience to motivate you to try to help you reach your potential. Even if I did, I wouldn't know where to start. Unless you are willing to try motivating yourself, it won't happen around here, and you will be the loser."

What, in your opinion, is wrong? What can Barry do to become a self-motivated professional? (For a suggested answer, see page 232.)

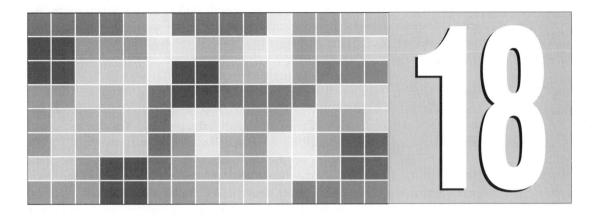

# Business Ethics, Rumors, and the Confidence Triangle

**"You call that ethical?"**

Thought for the Day: Don't underestimate the power of the golden rule that translates to: "treat others the way you want to be treated."

Dr. Albert Schweitzer once said: "In a general sense, ethics is the name we give to our concern for good behavior. We feel an obligation to consider not only our own well-being but also that of others and human society as a whole."

Business ethics involves being fully aware of what we are doing in the area of human relationships. Are we treating people the way they want to be treated? Are we complying with rules, such as the laws of the land, the customs and expectations of the community, the principles of morality, and the policies of the organization? Are we being true to ourselves?

Consider, for example, an honest employee who would never steal money from a cash box but who might use the company car to run personal errands while making sales rounds; or a high-producing, devoted employee who might work overtime in an emergency but tell his boss he got caught in traffic upon arriving late the next day when, in fact, he overslept; or a sympathetic employee who knows a co-worker is operating a small business on the side (often using company office equipment and paper) but says nothing.

Obviously, maintaining high ethical standards is not easy when co-workers may view the subject differently. Here are three attitudes that can help you throw off temptations and be true to yourself.

- *Respect company rules, procedures, and standards.* Remember, you can be unethical without breaking the law. Use common sense and assess the potential damage of an unethical act to your career. Violations are not worth it in the long run.

- *Be willing to test your ethical thinking frequently.* Ask yourself: "Is this the right thing to do? Is it fair? Is it honest? Am I creating a guilt feeling for nothing?"

- *Keep reminding yourself that relationships are built upon trust.* Unethical behavior can destroy relationships because it is difficult to respect an individual who flirts with accepted ethical standards.

Here are seven mistakes to avoid.

1. Misrepresenting the facts about my job activities or those of a co-worker.

2. Divulging personal or confidential information to co-workers, customers, competitors, or the general public.

3. Permitting, or failing to report, violations of any federal, state, or municipal laws or regulations.

4. Protecting unethical co-workers from corrective discipline.

5. Condoning or failing to report the theft or misuse of company property.

6. Covering up on-the-job accidents and failing to report health and safety hazards.

7. Passing on co-workers' ideas as your own.

# Rumors

*Webster's New World Dictionary* gives us this definition of rumor: "General talk not based on definite knowledge; mere gossip; hearsay; an unconfirmed report, story, or statement in general circulation."

All organizations have information collectors—employees who set up and maintain informal networks that keep them informed about what is going on at all times. An informal communication network is generally a harmless activity, provided that it doesn't interfere with the employee's personal productivity and is not used to spread rumors and malicious gossip.

Unauthenticated reports, or rumors, seem to originate and circulate within every group of people, especially when a group's members have common interests and competitive goals. Rumors are common in small communities, social and service groups, schools, churches, and, of course, business organizations.

Rumors are based on people's need to share their anxieties with others. Some rumors get started because of faulty communication or unintentional misinterpretation of the original message. Others consist of malicious gossip designed to hurt another person.

# Rumor Mills and Grapevines

Two popular expressions have become associated with the circulation of rumors. One is *rumor mill*. This familiar expression implies that rumors, like grain being processed in a mill, are turned out regularly in large numbers, altered, and circulated within the confines of a certain group or organization. Workers who are information collectors are all too frequently the chief providers of grist for the rumor mills.

The second popular expression is *grapevine*, which means an unofficial, confidential, person-to-person chain of verbal communication. The grapevine can best be viewed as an underground network that operates within an organization. The rumor mill may get the message started, but the grapevine keeps it moving. The grapevine has the reputation of operating without official sanction, and usually the information transmitted has an aura of secrecy.

Not all information that gets into the rumor mill and travels along the grapevine is false. It can be the truth. But the person who introduces the information must have the facts right, and those facts must be transmitted without misinterpretation. These conditions are, of course, seldom present. Even when the original information is accurate, facts can become distorted as they move along the grapevine.

The important thing to realize is that information processed through the rumor mill and passed along the grapevine is not reliable. It may not be based upon the facts. It may be slanted to serve the interests of a second, third, or fourth party. It may even be malicious.

For these reasons the rumor mill should be viewed with considerable caution, and information coming through the grapevine should be discounted. You cannot depend on it.

## Management's Position

Because rumors occur in all organizations, it is only natural to find them in business and industrial concerns. It follows that there may be a rumor mill in your organization. If there is, be forewarned. Accepting rumors as the truth can cause you to make serious human-relations mistakes. You might, for example, damage a good horizontal or vertical relationship you have built; or you might permit false information to get in the way of building a relationship that would contribute to higher productivity and, perhaps, enhance your own progress.

What is management's position to rumor mills? This book, of course, cannot speak for your particular management. However, we can say this: the term *rumor mill* is not new to those in leadership positions, and management usually knows when a grapevine exists.

We do not mean that the people responsible for management condone the grapevine, but they know when it is in operation. We know this because they occasionally step in and squelch a false rumor before damage is done to either an individual or the company. They might also deliberately leak some positive information into the grapevine so that employees will get an accurate message in a hurry.

You should realize that keeping employees fully informed on company matters through regular channels is a huge task. Conferences, bulletins, company periodicals, and other media are often not fully effective. But even if they were, it is doubtful that rumors would be eliminated. Management knows this. So if you are on the receiving end of rumors in your job, and you sense the existence of a rumor mill, do not let yourself believe that management is not concerned. It is!

## Employee's Position

Management is aware that unfounded rumors can cause unnecessary anxiety among employees and that such anxiety hurts the morale of the organization. Management also knows that rumors can sometimes be malicious and that innocent employees can be hurt. Management will do what it can to prevent harm to employees.

In order to be successful, however, management needs the help and support of every employee.

What might you do to help management? And, more important, what might you do to help yourself? Here are six suggestions.

1. *Admit that there is such a phenomenon as a rumor mill in your organization.* If you are blind to this situation, you may introduce and transmit harmful rumors to others without knowing it.

2. *All information received through the grapevine, especially if it has implications of intrigue, should be viewed with skepticism; and you should not permit grapevine information to disturb you personally.* If it is true, you will have time to adjust to it after you receive it from official sources. Be patient until you get the facts. Partial information is dangerous. Give management time to give you all the facts. Do not take any action or make decisions until you know.

3. *Do not be guilty yourself of introducing rumors into the grapevine.* You may, by accident, overhear something of a confidential nature and pass it on to someone as the truth, only to discover at a later date that you heard only part of the story. Or you may see something a little unusual and draw the wrong conclusion, as in the following case.

   **Rebecca.** Noticing her supervisor, a young married man, taking her co-worker, Florence, who was divorced, home two nights in succession, Rebecca decided something was going on between them. Without any malicious intent, Rebecca introduced the matter into the local grapevine; and, as so often happens, the rumor got out of hand. A number of people, including Rebecca herself, ended up hurt. The supervisor was transferred and his replacement was less effective. What was the truth? Florence had put her car in the repair shop for two days, and the supervisor had volunteered to take her home so that she would not have to walk the dark streets alone. Nothing more was involved.

4. *Refuse to pass on unsubstantiated information you receive secondhand.* If you don't pass on questionable secondhand information, you may break the circuit in the grapevine and perhaps keep others from being disturbed unnecessarily. For instance, sometimes during coffee-break talks, it may be possible to steer conversation away from rumors and onto harmless tracks, such as to sports or TV shows.

5. *If you must complain about company matters or company people, do so in the proper manner to your immediate supervisor, or blow off steam at home or with a trusted person—but not with your fellow workers.* Avoid complaining at work to eliminate the possibility of having your personal

gripes misinterpreted and introduced into the rumor mill. It will also keep anyone from using your complaints to hurt your relationship with your superiors.

6. *Try not to let a nonpersonal rumor that might involve your future with the company upset you until you get the facts.* If you do, there might be a noticeable drop in your personal productivity that will needlessly hurt your future. Make every effort to ignore a rumor until you receive official information. If you find you cannot keep from getting upset, consult your supervisor or someone else in management for the facts before you draw unwarranted conclusions. Many employees have injured their future by premature action based upon a false rumor. Don't fall into this trap.

## Personal and Nonpersonal Rumors

We could fill pages with examples and descriptions of the various kinds of rumors that travel along the grapevine. It will serve our purpose best, however, to place them all into the following two broad classifications.

Many on-the-job rumors involve *people's personal lives* and are not related to job situations. Some of these fall into the back-fence category. Some are little more than coffee-break gossip. Although there is considerable intrigue in such rumors, the new employee would be wise to keep working relationships strictly that—intrigue—and stay a safe distance from such rumors.

Rumors of the second kind concern the *organization.* They pertain to things that may or may not happen to the company. Although they influence employees, they are not personal. For example, there may have been rumors about layoffs, with no foundation in fact; rumors that departments were to be eliminated when in fact they were to be enlarged; rumors of resignations when in fact none were ever contemplated; and rumors of terminations that turned out to be transfers.

Organizational rumors have an enormous influence on the productivity of employees and the general progress of the company. Management, by keeping the official channels of communication open, tries to eliminate them. Rumors continue to exist in most companies, however. Unless employees develop a way to insulate themselves against rumors, they can become constantly insecure about their jobs and their future. Their personal productivity will go up and down based upon the latest rumor. And all for nothing!

## Confidence Triangle

Let's now look closely at one aspect of the problem from a positive point of view. Have you ever heard the expression *confidence triangle?* A confidence triangle is the way a confidential comment can be transmitted to a third party. The following description and diagram will help explain the idea.

We will assume that you are Mr. A. You have a strong, healthy relationship with Mr. B. Occasionally you talk things over with him in confidence. One day at lunch you mention that Mr. C has been of great help to you in completing a certain project and that you have considerable respect for his ability and perception.

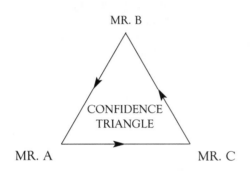

You do not realize, when you say this, that Mr. C has a strong, healthy relationship with Mr. B and that your comments will be transmitted to him. Of course, this will not hurt your relationship with Mr. C. In fact, it will improve it, because the favorable comments have been made in confidence and transmitted by a person Mr. C respects.

So far, the confidence triangle has worked in a positive manner. *But what if your comments had been negative?* Instead of improving your relationships with Mr. B and Mr. C, you would have damaged them. The confidence triangle works both ways. The truth is, then, that you can strengthen or weaken relationships with some people through others. When you say something positive about a third person to an individual with whom you have good rapport, relationships can improve. When you say something negative, the opposite can happen.

Nobody likes to accept advice. Even when advice comes at the right time from the right person in the right way, it is difficult to accept. Yet, sometimes accepting advice is the smart thing to do.

Let us assume that at this very moment the conditions are ideal and you are willing to accept advice. What might be the best human-relations advice you could receive? In all probability it would be this:

*If you can't say something good about a person, don't say anything at all.*

Like most advice that comes in such simple terms, this precept is far easier to state in print than to put into practice. Yet the degree to which you observe this simple rule on your new job will have considerable influence on your success.

Understanding the nature of rumors, the power of the rumor mill, the scope of the grapevine, and the impact of the confidence triangle should teach you to be very careful about what you say to others.

It has been said that many human-relations problems are self-created. There is truth in this statement.

> *Only with humor,*
> *consider a rumor;*
> *Be matter of fact,*
> *with ethics intact.*

# Case 18

**"Me? Fall for a rumor?"**

# Dilemma

When Sylvia began her new job as a human relations specialist, she was very optimistic about her future. After all, she was young, serious-minded, well educated, and capable. More than anything else she wanted a management role with her company.

Sylvia worked extremely hard for three years, and she did an excellent job in human relations. Her personal productivity was never questioned. Ms. Rogers, her supervisor, encouraged her to prepare to take over her job. She helped Sylvia considerably in this respect, but, of course, she could make no promises.

One day, Coleen, a close friend of Sylvia's who worked in another department of the company, shared some rather disturbing news with her. Coleen had heard that a Mr. Young, an employee from another department, was being trained to take Ms. Rogers's place as department head.

Although she said nothing and did not show it on the outside, Sylvia was very distressed by the news. It was hard to believe that management could make such a decision so long before announcing a promotion for Ms. Rogers. Sylvia fretted about the news constantly and could not keep her mind on her work. As a result, she made more and more mistakes, and several important reports were turned in late. Over the next six months, the excellent relationship she had with her supervisor slowly deteriorated.

Then, just as Coleen had said, top management made an official announcement that Ms. Rogers was promoted and Mr. Young was made department head. Sylvia was deeply hurt and disappointed.

What mistakes did Sylvia make that might have contributed to her ultimate disappointment? (For a suggested answer, see page 232.)

# PART V

# Success at Expanding
# Your Assets

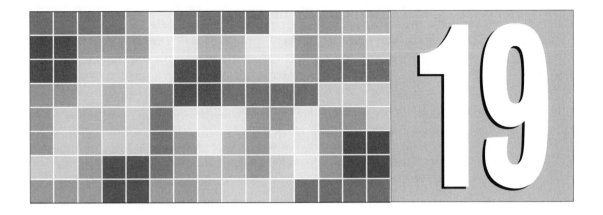

# Goal Setting
# and Attitude

**"Must I have a goal?"**

Thought for the Day: With enthusiasm and energy, ignite your fire to reach the goals that are important to you.

If you were to survey your friends, you would probably discover that those with the most positive attitudes have important goals they want to reach. Why does having goals make them more positive? One reason is that goal-oriented people are so involved in reaching their goals that they don't have the time or inclination to focus on negatives. Here are three examples of people who became more positive when they set new goals for themselves.

**Hector.**    A government employee, Hector was dragging along with little self-motivation and a negative outlook when he and his wife took a vacation at a nearby mountain resort. When it was over, they had a motivating goal: They wanted to earn and save money for a mountain cabin for getaway weekends. From that moment on, Hector had a more positive attitude.

**Cheryl.**    An office employee with a large corporation, Cheryl showed excellent potential but little interest in improving her career. Then, after taking a seminar on empowerment, she decided it was foolish to waste her potential. She decided she wanted to become a manager. Within days Cheryl's co-workers noticed an improvement in her attitude.

**Darryl.**    After ten years in a career that bored him, Darryl decided that a change was needed. His first step was to return to college for a higher degree. Once involved, he became so motivated that he started to look at his present job in a different light. Result? He lost his boredom and received a promotion before he earned his degree.

Obviously, there is a connection between goals and having a more positive outlook. What about you? Are you as goal-oriented as you should be? Would giving yourself one or two new goals improve your attitude, lead you to greater career success and eventually more personal fulfillment? Here are three factors to consider.

## Set Realistic Goals

*Realistic goals can give you a more positive outlook.*

We have defined attitude as the way you mentally look at things. Without goals, you are not heading anywhere. There is little or no *expectation!* With no direction and no expectations, it would be easier for you to talk in a negative way, think negative thoughts, and *become* a negative person.

**Adelle.**    Making excellent progress in becoming a high school science teacher, Adelle is handling her most difficult courses with relative ease. Adelle is an out-going person, yet somewhat self-conscious because she is about forty pounds overweight. When two of her friends convinced her to join them in an on-campus exercise and weight-loss program, Adelle gave herself a new goal. Along with earning her degree, she would lose the forty pounds and give herself a new image. What happened? Because of her new goal, she not only lost weight but improved her grades. Without knowing it, she needed a new, more challenging goal to improve her attitude.

# Reward Yourself

*Rewards for reaching goals are attitude-booster pumps.*

Many people, in establishing goals, underestimate the value of giving themselves rewards for making progress. Goals that do not provide rewards along the way are often forgotten. But when daily, weekly, and long-term rewards are attached, goals can have a major influence on attitudes. Consider this story about Drake.

> **Drake.**   With three years of experience on a police force, Drake decided to become a lawyer. Encouraged by his chief, he was given daytime schedules so he could take night classes. Drake figured it would take him five years before he would be in a position to take the bar exam. Thinking only about his long-term goal, which seemed mearly an impossible dream, Drake became so discouraged the first year that he almost gave up. It was then that he realized he needed a weekly goal to keep him motivated. Drake remembered how he enjoyed the volleyball team while attending college. When he discovered there was a Sunday volleyball game at the YMCA near where he lived, he knew he had found what he needed. In the future, he would do a professional job as a police officer during the day, attend classes and study at night and on Saturday, and designate Sunday as reward day. How did it work out? Drake passed the bar examination in four years instead of five.

# Balance Your Goals

*The right balance of immediate and long-term goals works best for most people.*

Each individual needs to design a goal "pattern" that produces the best results and attitude over the long term. Cameron provides us with an excellent example.

> **Cameron.**   Now 32 years of age and in a middle management position with a large utility firm, Cameron was asked to state the most important thing he had learned in college. His reply: "This may sound strange, but looking back, it was learning how to organize myself. I had many goals. First, of course, was earning a good GPA. I had some tough courses, so I had to concentrate. Then I needed some work goals because I had to pay my own way, and I wanted to establish myself as a responsible worker so that I could qualify for the best opportunity upon graduation. I also had exercise and diet goals. I worked out in the gym three or four times each week. To reach all of these goals took organization. I had a study schedule with specific goals for each course. Each Sunday I would write out my goals for the following week.
> But I was a senior before I learned about my need for the most important goals of all. With so much study, work, and exercising, I forgot that

I also needed fun time to balance things out. Result? I set aside every Saturday for pure pleasure purposes. I would play some basketball during the day and go dancing at night. Frankly, it was my weekly pleasure goal that pulled me through.

"Today I try to maintain a balance between career, family, and pleasure goals. You ask if there is a relationship between keeping an upbeat attitude and having goals? My answer is an emphatic "yes."

People need to get to know themselves well enough to discover which goals are motivating and how many are required to maintain their upbeat attitudes. As part of the motivation process, they also need to discover whether they respond best to daily, weekly, or long-term career and life goals, and in what combination.

- *Daily goals.* Creating and maintaining a dally checklist of tasks works well for those who want a feeling of accomplishment each day. For many, the feeling is all the reward needed. Others reward themselves with simple pleasures such as watching television, taking a walk, or eating a special kind of dinner or dessert.

- *Weekly goals.* Interviews indicate that a large number of people create weekly goals for themselves (usually on Sunday) and then reward themselves the following Saturday with special leisure events such as a game of golf, a movie, or a short trip. Almost all of them claim that leisure goals (rewards) work best to keep them upbeat on the job during the week.

- *Long-term goals.* Annual goals, such as taking a vacation trip, are motivating for some people. Career and life goals, on the other hand, are often vague and nonmotivating. It is, however, easy to defend the premise that those fortunate enough to have such goals live a more positive life—as long as the longer goals are realistic and meaningful and are *supplemented with shorter ones.*

Lifestyles that meet the needs of individuals and produce happiness and fulfillment are usually built around a combination of highly individualized goals. People with spouses or partners have the challenge of working out goals that satisfy both individuals while giving each other the freedom to build a few of his (or her) own.

**Janette.**     Because Janette and her husband did not succeed in designing a lifestyle that contained goals suitable to both of them, Janette found herself a single parent. For the first two years after their separation, Janette's three goals were to raise their daughter in the best way she knew how, make progress toward her career, and accomplish housekeeping chores so she and her daughter could do some fun things together. Everyone was surprised by her upbeat attitude—at least for awhile. But, as time went on, Janette became more and more negative. What was missing?

Through the help of a close friend, Janette finally realized that she needed time for a leisure goal. By working out an arrangement with her parents, Janette was able to leave her daughter with them on Sundays so she could have some free time for herself or to share with friends away from all responsibilities. The new arrangement provided the right combination of goals, and within weeks Janette regained her positive attitude.

For some reason, people of all ages are blind to their need to have some quality time for themselves. They become so involved in career, family, and household goals that they forget to establish a leisure goal that provides the balance required for a positive attitude.

To discover more about goals and your attitude toward them, complete the following exercise.

---

### RATE YOURSELF AS A GOAL-ORIENTED PERSON

This exercise is designed to help you review your attitude toward the advantages of setting goals for yourself. Please read each statement and then place a check mark in the appropriate box. The scoring procedure is explained below.

| | Yes | No | Undecided |
|---|---|---|---|
| 1. Do you feel you are more positive when you are reaching for a goal? | ❏ | ❏ | ❏ |
| 2. Does a day go better for you when you wake up with a goal to achieve? | ❏ | ❏ | ❏ |
| 3. Do you think it is a good idea to write out daily and weekly goals? | ❏ | ❏ | ❏ |
| 4. Do you believe each goal should have a reward attached to it? | ❏ | ❏ | ❏ |
| 5. Do you feel better at the end of the day when you have accomplished something you set out to do? | ❏ | ❏ | ❏ |
| 6. Do you feel goals are beneficial, whether they are reached or not? | ❏ | ❏ | ❏ |
| 7. Would your friends recognize you as a goal-oriented person? | ❏ | ❏ | ❏ |

|  | Yes | No | Undecided |
|---|:---:|:---:|:---:|
| 8. Are you convinced that goal-oriented people are more positive? | ❏ | ❏ | ❏ |
| 9. More than anything else, do goals help you live up to your potential? | ❏ | ❏ | ❏ |
| 10. Are goals worth having, even if they might cause frustration and disappointment if not reached on time? | ❏ | ❏ | ❏ |

TOTAL POINTS

Each "Yes" answer is worth 3 points. Each "Undecided" answer is worth 1 point. Each "No" answer is worth 0 points. If you scored 20 points or higher, you are enthusiastic about setting goals and feel they contribute to your positive attitude. If you scored between 10 and 20 points, you recognize the importance of goals in keeping an upbeat attitude. If you scored below 10 points, it would appear that you prefer to live with few, if any, goals and can stay positive in other ways.

Individuals who become effective goal-setters and achievers usually get a head start by becoming excellent personal time planners while still in school. Eduardo, a successful 43-year-old executive explains as follows:

> College taught me a lot of things but nothing more valuable to my career than personal time management. I had to juggle six balls at the same time—attend a full load of classes, schedule study hours, allocate twenty hours per week for my part-time job, arrange time for physical exercise and personal tasks such as washing, get enough sleep, and save some time for leisure or fun. To balance everything was no easy challenge. I've been a good planner ever since!

Whether in or out of high school or college, in your first job, or well established in your career, good time management involves:

- listing and prioritizing weekly goals;
- making and using a daily "to do" list;
- concentrating on what you are doing at the time; and
- saving a few hours for pure leisure activities.

An additional factor of consideration associated with goal-setting and planning can be summed up in a single sentence: *The absence of effective goal-setting and personal time management can result in confusion and cause an individual to lose her (or his) positive attitude.*

Only you can decide the direction best for you. But if you wish to become a more confident, positive, and successful person in your own individual style, giving more attention to goals may be your best approach. Keep in mind that all goals that produce results come from within the individual. People seldom succeed in imposing goals on others.

> *The journey through life is most successful when driven by goals.*

## Case 19

**"I need to find myself."**

# Conflict

Deric and RayLyn will graduate from their university in a few months. They have been romantically involved for almost two years. Deric is capable and popular, and shows great promise of succeeding in any career he selects (his major is sociology). But so far, he is not heading in any direction. When it comes to the future, he often appears confused and listless. RayLyn, on the other hand, is highly goal-oriented. She knows she is going to be a civil engineer, she wants children (one or two) by the time she is twenty-eight, and she is anxious to work out a lifestyle with the right partner. Hopefully, it will be Deric.

Last night, in what started out as a casual discussion, RayLyn lost her patience with Deric. Why? Because he got on his old theme of taking a one or two-year moratorium upon graduation so he could "find himself" before making any career or relationship commitments. RayLyn responded: "I know myself. I need to be headed somewhere. It's not ambition or money or anything else—it's just the way I stay positive. I have to have reachable goals ahead of me. I wouldn't be comfortable or happy trying to build a life with a person who avoids specific goals."

"Fine," replied Deric. "When it comes to goals, I may feel as you do in a few years, but I'm not sure. I don't want, at this time of my life, a goal-oriented existence. So far, I've pretty much done what my parents and society expect. It's time for me to live a life of pure freedom. You go your way, I'll go mine. Perhaps in a few years we can get back together and create a lifestyle that would bring fulfillment to both of us."

What chance do Deric and RayLyn have of restoring their relationship? Should they try? Will Deric eventually come to view goals differently? (For a suggested answer, see page 232.)

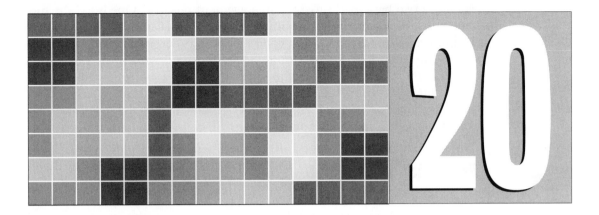

# Two Routes to the Top

**"I hate decision making."**

Thought of the Day: A positive attitude can make a "world of difference" in making decisions and achieving success.

There are two basic paths to a top management position. One is to join and stay with a large organization, climbing the ladder of success rung by rung. The other is to move from one company to another, improving your position with each move. Those who prefer to move up within the same organization are *stabilizers*. Those who prefer the zigzag route are *scramblers*.

If you go about it in the right way, you can usually build a rich and rewarding career as a stabilizer. The practice that makes this possibility attractive is called *promotion from within*, or *PFW*.

## Promotion from Within

Promotion from within (PFW) is an old practice in many companies. That is, there is nothing new about PFW. It has always been the custom to move those who demonstrate that they are capable and responsible into higher positions when vacancies occur. If effective people are available, management usually wants to promote from within the company's own ranks. A PFW policy encourages loyalty, provides some security, and has other advantages. It should be remembered, however, that even companies that have such a policy may make exceptions on their own or can be forced into adjustments because of layoffs and reorganizations.

In order to understand the implications of the PFW idea in a given corporation, one must study the organizational structure. Each company has grown to maturity in a different way; each firm has developed a different "culture." Every company has its own interpretation and application of a PFW policy.

Because of the wide disparity in business organizations and practices, generalizations are dangerous. The reader must interpret the following pages in light of the policies and practices of her (or his) own company. It is important, however, to give the new worker a perspective on the employee's career possibilities. The following triangle will get us started.

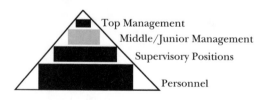

The diagram above could represent a business or an industrial or a governmental organization. Size is not important. It could be a company with 200,000 employees or one with 200 or even 15. Management—those people who are responsible for the leadership and direction of the company—is, of course, at the apex of the triangle. Some organizations divide management into three classifications: top management, middle/junior management, and supervisory positions. In recent years many organizations have eliminated middle/junior management positions primarily to remain competitive and profitable. As organizations have become flatter, front-line supervisors have had to assume more responsibilities. The elimination of many managerial positions also has pushed decision making to lower levels.

Top-management executives with giant concerns are usually the president and vice-presidents. Middle-management people are usually division heads, branch and plant managers, and management assistants. Supervisors are next in line.

Below the management level are many kinds of personnel, depending on the type of organization. In a manufacturing business, we find different levels of technical people: engineers, technicians, skilled craftsmen, semi-skilled workers, and helpers. In other kinds of organizations, there are different patterns and different backgrounds.

Supervisory positions, as illustrated here, usually outnumber higher-management positions. A supervisor for every 12 employees in an organization is quite common; however, it is not uncommon to have a lower or higher employee-supervisor ratio, such as a supervisor for 5- to 30-plus employees, depending on the type of business. The supervisory position is extremely important to the new worker; for in most cases, this is the first position leading to upper management.

Now that we have seen the top of the triangle, let us look at the bottom. All organizations employ the majority of new workers at lower-level entry positions.

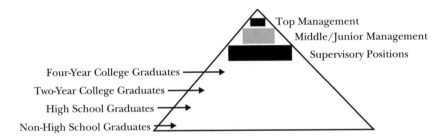

Not all companies have four entry levels. Some have only one, two, or three. For example, some organizations may hire only four-year college graduates with specialized degrees. Other companies may seek employees who have experience or special skills. The important thing is that all employees have an opportunity to grow. Each employee, regardless of where he (or she) starts, can and should move up in the organization. Moving up the career ladder in an organization is the meaning of PFW.

## Pros and Cons of PFW

There are both advantages and disadvantages to building a lifetime career as a stabilizer in a single organization. Those who join companies with PFW intentions usually compete with those inside the company for better positions. They need not worry so much about outsiders who might be hired to fill positions to which they aspire. Theoretically, everyone has a chance to compete, despite differences in education and experience. When someone at the top retires, a chain reaction can open up many positions all the way down the organizational ladder. Several position openings, of course, are possible only if reorganization does not take place or certain positions are not eliminated.

Organizations with PFW policies usually provide good training for their employees, so that they are ready to assume more responsibility when opportunities arise. Because on-the-job time is spent on training of all kinds, it also usually means that such companies will encourage their employees to continue their formal education and will often pay for tuition. As a result, employees are less likely to be ignored or lost in the shuffle.

Just as there are many advantages, there are also disadvantages working for a company that likes to promote from within. Many highly ambitious people claim that promotions come too slowly. People are trained too far ahead of time. There is too much waiting. These are usually the same people who claim that the best way to reach the top is to move from company to company instead of staying with one organization. They point out that it is also possible that while waiting for an opening, a reorganization can take place, thus eliminating the position you were preparing to occupy. Moreover, the human-relations role is more critical because management and nonmanagement people seldom forget anything. *In short, a person who makes a serious human-relations mistake in a PFW company must live with it longer because the people affected will be around to remember.*

In the rapidly changing technological and global economic climate, organizations realize that they must be more flexible if they are to remain profitable. In some cases, restructuring and massive layoffs have been necessary. As a result, the emphasis on PFW is much reduced; in some organizations, it has been discarded.

## Zigzag Approach

The scrambling, or zigzag, route to the top involves an entirely different approach to career planning, as you can see from the following illustration.

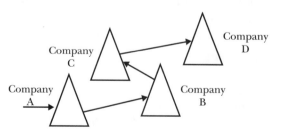

Just as there are advantages and disadvantages to the PFW approach to the top, there also are pros and cons to a zigzag approach.

One of the advantages of the zigzag or scrambling approach may be for a person to be promoted quickly. That is, for those who are willing to move about geographically and who are sufficiently aggressive to make the effort to seek out profitable transfers, the route to the top can be faster. Sometimes an individual can achieve a wider and more valuable learning background by moving from one company to another. In other words, she (or he) can learn something new in each company and take it to the next one. Increasing one's expertise by moving from one company to another is especially true in high-technology fields.

Another advantage to the scrambling approach is that it is easier to leave serious human-relations mistakes behind. Getting a fresh start in a new company might include leaving behind unresolved human conflicts or personality differences.

There are also disadvantages to the zigzag route. Most people agree that it takes more energy to build an industrywide reputation to ensure that profitable transfers come your way. There is also a degree of risk involved. You could discover, for example, that your most recent move was a mistake. Scramblers are not always successful.

Transferring often means uprooting the entire family and making profound personal and social, as well as professional, changes in your life. Certain benefits, like profit sharing, cannot always be transferred from one company to another without loss or adjustment. Also, during periods of recession, when layoffs occur in many organizations, scrambling becomes more difficult and risky. Thus, with the zigzag approach to career building, it is a good idea to do extra research and exercise more caution than you might do with a more conservative approach.

## Career Planning Factors

As you plan your career, take the following seven human-relations factors into consideration.

1. The longer you stay with a growing company, the more opportunities you will have, provided that you continue to learn and maintain good horizontal and vertical relationships.

2. Moving horizontally into every possible department in an organization is a good idea, even if the move does not give you an immediate pay increase. Not only will you improve your knowledge base, but you will also be in a position to build new relationships that can help your career progress.

3. Discover and study the various channels of promotion in your company. Attempt to move up through the channel that best suits your ability. Set the stage for promotion through your human-relations skills.

4. Within bounds, do not fear being aggressive. Submit ideas that have been well researched. Communicate upward. Demonstrate your human-relations skills at every opportunity.

5. When a position becomes vacant, let management know in the right way that you are interested. Do not assume that they know. It doesn't hurt your relationships with others to ask.

6. Cultivate and maintain relationships outside your organization, especially with people in professional or trade organizations. If it becomes obvious that your organization cannot provide you with the growth opportunities you desire, these individuals can help you scramble.

7. Keep in mind that the training you receive as an employee (whether as a stabilizer or a scrambler) may be preparing you to enter a new career in an emerging field or to open a business of your own. Entrepreneurship is continuing to grow and is experiencing rapid growth in most parts of the world. E-commerce and improving communication technologies are creating exciting opportunities for all types of people, especially entrepreneurs.

## Working Environments

It usually takes a few weeks before new employees are in a position to analyze their working environments and answer the following questions: Does this working environment (culture) fit my long-term needs? Is it within my personal comfort zone? Can I see myself moving up into more responsible positions?

In evaluating a working environment, the following issues need to be taken into consideration:

- Is there a profit-sharing or stock-option plan that causes employees to stay longer and be more protective of their respective roles and of the firm as a whole?

- How stable is the organization? Is the firm strong enough to withstand a takeover attempt by an outside firm? Is management sufficiently flexible to adjust to the economic winds of change?

- Is there a career class system within the organization? For example, hospitals have their medical doctors at one level, nurses at another, and non-professionals at another. Would you be comfortable in a similar environment?

- Would it bother you to work for an organization (e.g., a restaurant) in which the steady turnover of employees makes it difficult to build long-term relationships?

■ What about off-hours, shift, or overtime work? Hospitals, restaurants, and many factories have shift work that can have a major impact on one's lifestyle. Working for an airline, a hotel, or a travel agency also can mean longer-than-usual hours (paid or non-paid) than a regular business-hours position would require.

■ Would working in a high-fashion environment be within your comfort zone? Some retail organizations and home office centers create a haute couture environment that some enjoy but others do not.

Although the more investigation that takes place in advance the better, many new employees discover that the working environment they antici-pated is not suitable for them. As a result, they develop a new career plan that will eventually take them into their comfort zone.

# Plan B

The professional scrambler always has an alternative plan, or a Plan B, that he (or she) can put into operation when needed.

Having a Plan B is similar to a company that has a business plan. The company has a vision and mission for its future. It has strategies to achieve its goals. Its business plan describes what the company does, where it plans to go, and how it will get there. By developing your "personal" business plan, you identify your career (and personal) goals and the viable routes you may take to reach your mission. The best Plan B, as part of a personal business plan, includes a well-thought-out strategy (including an up-to-the-minute re-sume, outside contacts, and constantly updated skills) that will permit the scrambler to locate a better position with another firm in the shortest pos-sible time.

For the most part, in years past, stabilizers did not feel the need to have a Plan B. There are two reasons why a single career plan is no longer viable. First, stabilizers have discovered that scramblers have often substantially im-proved their career positions by having and using an alternative plan. Sec-ond, organizational changes (mergers, buy-outs, restructuring, etc.) have frequently left stabilizers holding the bag. The result? More and more sta-bilizers are going back to school to upgrade their skills and develop a for-mal Plan B as part of their personal business plan.

Both scramblers and stabilizers can benefit from developing a Plan B, basically for two reasons:

1. If the winds of change eliminate your position, you are prepared to move on to something better.

2. Having a Plan B ready makes it easier for you to maintain a positive at-titude where you are presently working.

Many workers become either discouraged with their progress or fearful that their jobs will be eliminated without doing anything about it. When they develop a personal business plan (which includes several alternative routes, such as a Plan B or C, to reach career goals), they not only eliminate some of the fear that goes along with losing a job, but they also feel better about their current positions. As a direct result, their attitudes improve, they become more productive, and they receive promotions. With so many positive factors in their favor, there really is no need to scramble.

> *Having a career alternative could help stablize the wind beneath your wings should you be forced from your perch.*

# Case 20

**"I'm a stabilizer."**

# Preference

Angelo, an experienced wireless equipment technician, had been promoted to manage a technical division in his organization because of his demonstrated technical and human-relations skills. However, due to a major restructuring at his company when it entered the e-commerce arena, his position was eliminated and he was forced into the labor market. Angelo was interviewed the same week by Company A and Company B, two high profile e-businesses. It took nearly three weeks for both of the firms to "check out" Angelo's background. The result was that both companies offered him a job, but both were lower-paying positions than Angelo had had in his previous position.

Company A is a dynamic high-technology corporation that makes little effort to develop its own people. In fact, it takes great delight in hiring top people away from its competitors. Company A is interested in Angelo primarily because of his technical skills and the fact that he would become productive immediately.

Company B, on the other hand, is a technical organization that offers a lot of security to employees because of its rather firm PFW policy. They like Angelo because of his technical abilities, but especially because of his long-range potential for management.

Although the starting salary with Company A is substantially higher, the training program with Company B is superior. *All other significant factors are similar.* In which company do you think Angelo should accept a position? What factors should he consider in making his decision? (For a suggested answer, see page 233.)

# Keeping a Positive Attitude Through Plateau Periods and Reorganizations

*"It's hard enough during regular times."*

Thought for the Day: Appreciate the rules of the road—caution, stop, and go—as you keep a watchful eye on the important targets in life.

Keeping a positive attitude takes on a new dimension when an ambitious employee reaches a plateau period in her (or his) climb up the corporate ladder. (A *plateau* is a long waiting period in which the role and the responsibility of the employee remain static.) Small automatic or cost-of-living pay increases may occur, but significant jumps do not. Sometimes plateau periods can last for years.

Why are plateaus so difficult to live through?

In the first place, business and industry seem to intensify the problem because they seek out and hire highly ambitious people. They want and need dynamic men and women. They want and need people with energy. And they often imply, but give no assurances, that personal progress will be swift and regular. Consequently, after hiring these ambitious people, it is often necessary to turn around and ask them to be patient.

"It takes time in any organization, Laura. Your day will come. Just sit tight and *wait.* You'll see."

"You are doing great, Joe. Just *wait* for the right opportunity, and you'll be off and running."

"Continue to prepare, Henry. Learn all you can in your present job. You are in a plateau period, but you will get your chance. Just *wait* and see."

## Learning Patience

Sometimes the "patience suit" that management suggests other employees wear during plateau periods becomes too tight, too confining, and too uncomfortable. When this happens, even confirmed stabilizers may consider scrambling to another firm.

Patience isn't something one learns in school or college. Indeed, the pattern of almost automatic promotions in school is the direct opposite of the pattern found in the world of work. Through our school systems, people become accustomed to promotions according to age. They start at the first grade and move up to the twelfth and beyond like clockwork— each year a step up, until regular promotions are expected without waiting. Small wonder that some people begin to think that life is one progressive step after another, whether the step has been truly earned or not.

Our society contributes in other ways to the "make it in a hurry" attitude. For example, both economic and social upward mobility have been the pattern for most Americans in the past few generations. As a result, most young people whose parents have "made it" have been raised in an affluent environment. Why should they wait for thirty years to get to the same point? Why should they wait until they're ready to retire to reach the higher rungs of the ladder, when they might do it by the time they're thirty?

Yet, when they get their first job, many young people must start at the bottom. Many start with a relatively low income and no fixed promotion schedule upon which to depend. Small wonder that many become impatient and seek shortcuts to better positions and higher incomes.

## Why Plateaus?

There are many reasons for plateau periods. The following quotations from three ambitious individuals are examples.

"I work for a fine company, but we have been undergoing unavoidable retrenchment for over three years. There has been a freeze on new hires and promotions. I think things will open up soon but, believe me, it has not been easy to readjust my personal goals and keep my attitude from showing."

"In our organization, everyone must sweat out a long plateau between management levels. I have had three front-line supervisory roles over the past few years, each with more responsibility. My next jump will be into middle management. But there are many people waiting ahead of me. If I could make a move to a competing company, I might save myself a few years of waiting."

"I was all set to move into a role I had spent three years preparing for when my organization went through a consolidation period. The position I wanted was transferred to another city. Not wishing to move there, I had to readjust my goals. So here I am, in another plateau period."

## Coping with Plateaus

Even if things could be normal in business organizations, which is seldom the case, promotions are not automatic. Plateaus still exist. So how is one to cope?

First, the ambitious employee should learn as much as possible about plateaus so that he (or she) can see the value of staying positive during such periods. Second, the employee should study ways in which such periods can be shortened.

Business and industrial leaders believe in *promotion by merit*. They know that the opportunity to succeed in open competition with others provides the vitality their organizations must have. Seniority, experience, minority status, and age are not always enough to warrant a promotion. Capability must also be demonstrated. But even the most capable employees reach plateaus. The opportunities to move up still exist, of course, but they sometimes come only after long periods of waiting.

Periods of waiting for promotions are critical, can destroy confidence, and can create problems. But far more important than all other factors is what happens to the attitude of the employee during such periods of waiting. Here is what frequently happens.

*When employees who are living through a plateau period permit their attitudes to turn negative, they defeat themselves.* At the very point when management is watching and they should be working up to their potential, they let things fall apart. When things unravel, the plateau is often extended, and others, who have better control of their attitude, are given the promotional opportunities that exist. Another way of saying this is that an ambitious employee cannot afford the "luxury of being bored."

It is not easy to ask an aggressive person to remain positive and wait, but often there is no alternative. Opportunities can and do open up in organizations overnight, but it is almost impossible to produce a steady flow of opportunities to fit the time schedules of individuals.

Management cannot eliminate all the pressure points that are faced by an employee stuck on a plateau. Management people can, however, understand the frustration that comes when a promising career gets temporarily bogged down. They know because they have usually been there themselves. They know it is a difficult period. They know it is a time when some people begin to seriously question their goals. They know it is a time when personal values are challenged. They know it is a time when some start to think about other careers or returning to college for more formal education.

Being ambitious and capable has never been easy in our society. When employees are in their twenties, a year may seem more like five years. And yet many employees are past thirty before they are given an opportunity to demonstrate fully their true ability.

True, a few people do find success early. The entertainment field, professional sports, sales, and promotional activities, for example, may give an early break to the young person who has talent, ability, and desire. Also, starting a business of one's own may offer the success an ambitious person may need.

While at first it may appear that professional people also achieve their goals early in life, it is easy to forget that those who build careers in medicine, engineering, law, and the other professions must invest considerable time in their formal education. Many physicians are often 30 years of age or older when they start their practices. The same is true for lawyers, engineers, and many other professionals.

## Reducing Plateau Periods

Understanding plateau periods may help an ambitious employee do a better job of coping, but aren't there ways to shorten them? Should you be faced with a plateau period in the future, ask yourself these questions:

- Am I using my present role to improve my future, whether or not I stay with the organization?

Some people have the capacity to turn boring jobs into self-improvement periods. A good example is the ambitious supervisor of a shipping operation who wants to know more about data processing. On company time, she (or he) might start investigating the possibilities for her own department, thereby benefiting both her department and herself.

- Am I taking advantage of all the training opportunities available to me now?

Such opportunities could exist both inside and outside the company. Community involvement of any kind can help one live through or even shorten a plateau period. Many employees have found moonlighting both therapeutic and financially rewarding.

- Is it time to revise my career goals? Is it time to scramble?

When organizations change internally, employees must adjust. Instead of resisting changes, they must turn them into opportunities. For example, you might consider changing your channel of promotion by asking for a transfer to a growing, instead of a declining, department. Or even better, reassess your personal business plan, and, if needed, revise and put your Plan B to work (Review Chapter 20).

- Have I applied for a promotion?

Upward communication to let management know you feel you are ready for more responsibility is often worthwhile, even if nothing happens. It may not eliminate a plateau, but it could shorten it.

- Are there some company-sponsored activities in which I could become involved?

Often there are sports activities, study groups, and cultural programs that can give you additional employee and management contacts as well as pleasure. Such activities may not shorten plateau periods, but they may make them seem shorter.

■ What about doing something spectacular?

Can you volunteer for a very tough assignment that nobody else has been willing to tackle? A new assignment for which you volunteered could provide you with a personal challenge. It could also communicate a message to upper management about your potential and readiness to accept more responsibility.

## Plateau-Related Action Steps

There are many other action steps people can take to shorten plateau periods, or at least to make them easier to live through. There are also cases where the employee should not live through them but rather adopt the zigzag route to the top and initiate a move to another organization. In contemplating such action, keep the following three points in mind. They will help you remain positive.

1. *The first years with an organization should be viewed as an apprenticeship.* The training and experience must be considered the plus factors during this learning period. The employee is serving an internship similar to that in the medical profession.

2. *Many employees have received promotions before they were ready, and their careers have been permanently damaged.* Will you be sufficiently trained for a good opportunity when it does come? Will you be ready for the responsibility? Will you be sufficiently mature to handle it? "Too much too soon" could be a real threat to your long-range goal.

3. *Although few people question the fact that personal advancement is often slow during the starting years, they seldom point out that the tempo of personal progress can increase greatly in later years.* Thus, don't set up a rigid personal timetable for yourself. Progress may be slow at the start of your career but very fast later. Yes, set a goal for yourself, but do not expect that goal to arrive exactly according to your time schedule. It may not fit that of your organization.

If you do set your own time schedule and management is unable to meet it, you may end up losing your positive attitude. Reducing or losing your positive attitude will hurt you as well as the company. The future of any company cannot be charted in detail many years in advance.

Today, more than during any previous period in time, organizations are going through massive, serious restructuring. Sometimes such changes create waiting periods, cause reassignments, and even result in layoffs. At other times, reorganizations create opportunities for those alert enough to perceive them. Not all changes are predictable. Not all changes can be converted into career opportunities. But some can—and it is your job to be ready when they occur. Ready and waiting. Staying positive as you live through plateaus can be the greatest human-relations challenge you face. That is why more and more professionals are developing personal business plans.

> *A positive attitude will provide solid footing if a pause on the career ladder becomes longer than anticipated.*

# Case 21

**"I hate change."**

# Change

In a company-sponsored seminar on how to handle and adjust to change, Ingrid made this statement to the group: "When it comes to the future and the changes it may bring, I believe that the Protestant ethic of hard work plus sound human-relations techniques will see me through. If my present superiors do not recognize and reward me, then someone else will."

The following response came from Darla, a co-worker and good friend of Ingrid's: "I think it is commendable for Ingrid to have so much faith in hard work and human-relations skills, but I think that adapting to change requires a more aggressive and creative approach. Ingrid, with her somewhat naive attitude, may be left behind. It has been my practice to try to turn change into opportunity through action. When a change occurs, I sit back for a day or so and figure out how I can use the change to my advantage and enhance my career. At such a critical juncture, I cannot rely on past performance and routine human relations. I must shift gears and look out for number one, even if it means temporarily stepping on the feelings of others. When change comes, it is not business as usual. I cannot prevent or control change, but if I am clever, I can turn it to my advantage."

Who, in your opinion, is better prepared to handle the dramatic changes most experts claim will occur in the future, Ingrid or Darla? Is there a better strategy? (For a suggested answer, see page 233.)

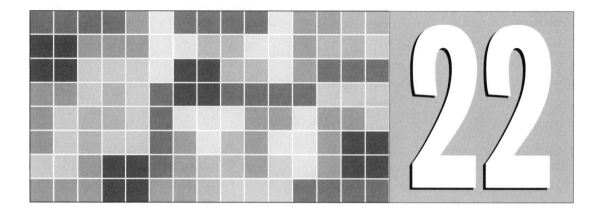

# When You Are
# Tempted to Scramble

**"I'm ready for a fresh start."**

Thought for the Day: Keep your house in order for you'll never know when your attitude and human relations skills will influence your future.

Freedom to accept or resign a job, seek employment in a certain career field, or join the organization of one's choice is an important right. It should be appreciated by all free people. What does this freedom mean to you, a member of the work force?

It means you can be a stabilizer and, provided that you select the right firm, you can build your entire career within a single organization. It means you can leave a position with a large or small organization and go into business for yourself. It means you can leave your present occupation and go back to school to prepare for a new career. It also means you may choose to become a scrambler and follow the zigzag route to the top by making a move to another organization every time you can substantially improve your situation. It means you can keep switching jobs until you find the occupation or company that's right for you.

## The Decision to Scramble

The temptation to scramble is reduced during periods of economic slowdown for two reasons: (1) more qualified people are unemployed and already in the marketplace, trying to capture the fewer positions available; (2) one is less tempted to make a geographical move in uncertain times when it may be more difficult to sell an existing home. Even so, intense scrambling continues as creative opportunities open up in smaller companies.

Some resignations are positive actions; they benefit both the organization and the individual. Some make sense because reorganizations increase the possibility of future layoffs. Some resignations, for a variety of personal reasons, are unavoidable. Others, however, seem to stem from poor judgment and turn out to be mistakes.

There are dangers to any resignation. You could wind up with a job that is not as good as the one you left. You might even wind up temporarily stranded. Thousands of people leave organizations every year, only to regret it later. The pastures in another occupational area or company may, from a distance, look greener than they really are. Resigning a position, whether you have a door open elsewhere or not, is a serious step. Careful research is recommended.

## Why Resign?

When should you resign a position?

As a general rule, you should resign when you have been *unhappy and unproductive for a considerable length of time.* Under such conditions, your career with the company has already been seriously damaged. A new start in a new environment would most likely be to your advantage.

People who are ambitious should look elsewhere for employment when they discover they have not been working close to their potential for a long time. They should seek opportunities elsewhere when their productivity has been down for months and they can't seem to improve it. They should consider other options when their attitude has been negative for a long time and they do not seem to be able to do anything about it.

Surveys and statistics show, however, that most resignations are not due to the preceding reasons.

*Most resignations are based primarily upon personality conflicts and human-relations problems.*

Rather than leaving for a better position, people are getting *away* from the frustrations of their present job. Because such problems can frequently be solved, or at least made less traumatic, it would appear that many people resign their positions for the wrong reasons. In other words, leaving a job because it is not the right one for you is one thing. Leaving a job because of human-relations incompetencies is something else.

To help you avoid these and other mistakes, here are some questions to ask yourself when considering a resignation.

■ Are you resigning under emotional stress?

We are all tempted to chuck a job when everything seems to be going wrong or when we are frustrated and upset. It is a natural reaction. A resignation, however, should be a rational decision based upon many facts, and should be made only after long, careful analysis and planning.

It is difficult to think clearly and logically when you are emotionally upset about a human-relations problem that cannot be quickly solved. During these periods, back away from such a serious decision. Sleep on it. Talk to another person. Give it time. Make another, more serious attempt to solve it. A resignation should not be an impulsive decision. In the majority of cases, it is irrevocable.

■ Are you resigning because of a personality conflict?

Resigning because of a single personality conflict can seriously hamper a promising career. This is not to say that such conflicts do not occur. They do. But they can usually be resolved with time and effort. Give someone in authority a chance to help. Give time a chance to help. Most of all, be honest with yourself and ask whether you can afford to let one person destroy a promising career—especially when it is yours.

■ Are you resigning because you feel your job may be eliminated?

Almost all organizations make adjustments during lean economic times. Rumors of staff reductions circulate from time to time. During such periods, smart employees dig in to make themselves more valuable so that they will be less vulnerable to layoffs. They also improve their skills and set in motion a Plan B should the rumors prove to be true. To resign a job during organizational adjustment periods can be a major mistake. Due to early retirement inducements, more responsible positions may become available for those who sit tight and continue to produce.

■ Are you marking time?

Frequently, highly capable employees sense that they are not going anywhere in their present jobs, yet they do nothing to find a better opportunity. Such individuals often drag along for years, doing a disservice to both themselves and their organizations. Later you hear them say: "I should have made a change years ago!" Facing such a negative career situation head on may be justified to avoid the penalties and regrets of lack of progress later.

■ Have you talked your situation over with your supervisor or the person who hired you?

Many employees are fearful about talking over a possible resignation with a management person. Some believe that it will be held against them if they voice their dissatisfaction. They feel that their chances of finding a better job elsewhere will be weakened. Some feel it would be an act of disloyalty. Others feel it to be a waste of time.

Whatever your reason, you would be wise not to resign until you have discussed the problem with your supervisor or someone in personnel or upper management. A twenty-minute discussion with the right person has stopped many a foolish resignation. Many problems can be resolved through free and open communication with management. Give those in charge a chance to help you resolve your problem before you take final action. You have nothing to lose. You could even discover that the position you are thinking of leaving has more potential than any you could find elsewhere.

■ Are you resigning to save face?

Everyone makes mistakes. Sometimes you may overcommit yourself or take a stand on an issue from which you feel you cannot back away. Resigning on this basis can be a mistake, especially if you have exaggerated the difficulty of the adjustment. It may be better to admit such a mistake than to pay a price that is out of all proportion. Such a resignation might be harmful to both your future and the company.

■ Have you exhausted all opportunities to learn more where you are?

A key factor in any decision to resign should be whether you can continue to grow in your present job. If you are completely boxed in, with no opportunity to improve yourself, then you should certainly consider a change. If however, you can continue to learn while waiting for a break, your situation is not as bad as it could be.

■ Are you working close to your potential?

Your future depends on your having a position in a company where you can work close to your potential. If the gap between what you are capable of doing and your current level of productivity is too wide, your career progress may be stalled. You must be able to use your ability, aptitude, and talent to a reasonable extent. You must be productive to succeed. You must find a way to contribute.

*Your company is entitled to the best in you.* If you find that your position doesn't bring out the best in you, then it isn't fair to either you or the company for you to remain. You should find something more suitable. Employees who are not productive are doing themselves and the company more harm than good.

## Resigning with Dignity

If, after serious consideration of all of the preceding questions you decide to resign in the best interests of all concerned, how should you go about it? Here are a few tips on how to resign gracefully.

*Resign on a face-to-face basis.* It is good human relations to go to the person who hired you, as well as to your supervisor, and resign face to face. A letter of resignation or a telephone resignation alone may leave a bad impression that could hurt you later. You will gain the respect of management when you resign in person. You will feel better, too.

*Tell management the real reasons for your resignation.* It may be difficult for you to reveal the actual causes for your leaving, but you should do so anyway. Reliable information of this kind can lead to changes that will benefit those you leave behind. Honesty is always the best human-relations policy.

*Give ample notice.* Be sure that you give at least the traditional two weeks' notice. If your company has a policy for tendering a resignation, follow it if at all possible. By following the policy, you could avoid damaging your present relationship with the company. Consider the company's position— a certain amount of time may be necessary for the company to recruit and train a replacement.

*Continue to be productive.* Don't take advantage of the fact that you are leaving. You will gain respect from others, as well as personal satisfaction, by working hard up to the very last hour. Continuing your productivity is one way to leave a clean record behind you.

*Turn in all equipment.* All company equipment, down to the most minute item, should be officially turned in through regular channels and be in the best condition you can leave it.

*Transfer all responsibilities to your replacement gracefully.* Give the person taking over your job a break. Give her (or him) all possible help and assistance. Try not to leave her with any problems you can take care of before leaving. Transfer to her, as far as possible, any good relationships you have developed.

*Swallow any last-minute negative comments.* There is a temptation for some people to become negative and pour out their hostilities before they have turned in their resignations. Resist any vindictive instincts you may have.

*Move on for the right reasons.* Those who move on for the right reasons— opportunity to use new knowledge, gain broader experience, improve career status and financial benefits—avoid the consequences of repeating human-relationship mistakes and communicating instability on their job applications.

*Always resign a position in such a manner that you will feel free to seek reemployment there at a later date.* You are the sum total of all your experiences. When you leave a job, you do not leave empty-handed. You take your experience and training with you. And you take the knowledge you've gained from all your human-relations experiences. Such knowledge is never without value. Make that known. Leave on the right basis.

To sum up our discussion on good advice when turning in a resignation, consider the following statement made by Kendall, a shopping center manager:

> One of the most important things I learned in college was to anticipate and be willing to accept change. I expected I would walk into a dynamic, changing world; I was not prepared for the turmoil that really exists. Many outstanding people are left unemployed through no fault of their own.

## Protect Your Positive Attitude

Like other things in life, organizations grow, decline, go through management shake-ups, and sometimes change ownership. The fear of a possible layoff, relocation, or adjustment to a new work environment and superior can turn an upbeat, productive employee into a negative one.

*How would you protect your positive attitude under the preceding circumstances?* Here are four important tips to help you stay positive as you contemplate a career change.

1. *Your positive attitude belongs to you, not to your company.* Your positive attitude is a priceless personal possession, so protect it for your own happiness. Keep in mind that a rumor about an organizational change is still a rumor until it has been verified and a definite change in your status has been made. Contrary to popular belief, the majority of ownership changes do not result in layoffs and significant adjustments among lower-level managers and employees.

2. *To help remain positive, start a Plan B.* Whether a forced change is coming or not, it is always a sound idea to explore other options through a Plan B (Refer to Chapter 20). Upgrade your skills where you are. Be a winner no matter what happens.

3. *Don't take organizational restructuring personally.* A company sale or change of ownership may appear to be a cold, calculated business decision, but it is transacted within the same free enterprise system in which the company was created and nurtured in the first place. It is unfortunate when job losses occur, but neither you nor anyone else is to blame. Focus on the fact that if you keep your positive attitude, a prospective employer will likely see you as a lucky find. Sometimes unwelcome change leads an individual with the right attitude to a superior career role.

4. *Your reputation is not damaged by corporate restructuring.* It does not hurt your reputation to be caught in a situation where an organizational change forces you into a career move. It is discouraging enough to go through any adjustment caused by a change in ownership. If you lose your positive attitude along with it, you are a double loser.

Finally, in a time of career change, particularly when the choice is not entirely yours, it is important to stay objective and professional. If it is to your advantage, go out and find yourself a more rewarding position!

> *To move mountains of uncertainty and change, you need to have the right attitude.*

# Case 22

## "Attitude makes the difference."

# Interview

Mark was quite discouraged when his job was eliminated. He was even more discouraged when, after seven job interviews in three months, he had no job offers.

Mark had tried extremely hard to get a job—he followed sound job seeking practices, did research on all the organizations before the interviews, was meticulous in his grooming, was careful in completing the application form, and always submitted a résumé.

What was wrong? Were economic conditions bad?

When Mark asked the opinion of a very perceptive placement director about his dilemma, together they came to the conclusion that Mark was not communicating well or transmitting his best attitude during the interview. While Mark had more than the minimum qualifications for all the positions for which he applied, he was losing out to other applicants.

Because Mark is a good friend of yours, you decide to help him out in developing answers (and a strategy to assure he is not too low key, too strong, too brief, nervous, phony, etc.) to the following four main questions he has been encountering in his interviews: (1) What made you decide that you would like to work for our company? (2) What do you feel you will be able to contribute to our organization? (3) What human-relations skills will you bring with you? and (4) What are some of your weaknesses?

Role play or write out, word for word, the way you would reply to each of the questions. (For suggested answers, see page 234.)

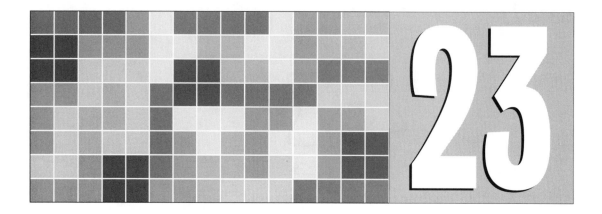

# Attitude Renewal

**"Something needs adjusting."**

Thought for the Day: If you give your positive attitude away by praising others and taking positive action, you'll reward yourself and everyone around you.

*Renewal* means to restore or refresh. Employees at all levels occasionally need to renew their positive view toward their careers, rejuvenate their approach to the type of work they perform, or reestablish their positive focus toward their organizations. Everyone, even the most optimistic individual, should, from time to time, go through some form of attitude renewal. To some, maintaining a positive focus is a full-time job.

## Attitudinal Rejuvenation

Attitude renewal, at the first level, is often a daily process. For a few, moments of early-morning meditation are helpful. Others, who may get off to a bad start, call a friend in mid-morning for a "boost" and then start the day anew. Other forms of adjustment (regaining a positive focus) can take place at other points throughout a given day.

At a more serious level, attitude renewal can be a weekend project. You hear both employees and managers make statements such as:

"I need a strong dose of weekend rest and recreation to get my attitude ready for Monday morning."

"Without the quiet time I enjoy during weekends, I would be a basket case Monday morning."

Without periodic time off or weekend attitude adjustment periods, most people could not remain positive and productive in their work environments.

There are times, however, when even weekend renewals are not sufficient. A major overhaul may be necessary. A major attitude overhaul may be needed because now and then most individuals fall into an "attitudinal rut."

An attitudinal rut usually occurs when someone slips unknowingly into a pattern of negative behavior that, unfortunately, can continue over a long period of time. Although some days are better that others, the individual's focus is permanently skewed to the negative side of his (or her) perception. Obviously, remaining in an attitudinal rut can inflict severe damage on one's career.

Nevertheless, it is possible to fall into such a rut without knowing it. When you become physically ill, for example, your body sends you a signal—you get a headache, a fever, or pain—and you do something about it. When you slip into an attitudinal rut, your mind may be unable to send you a clear signal of distress because it does not inflict physical pain. Your co-workers or close friends may *want* to send you a signal, but it is such a sensitive area that they back away. As a consequence, some people stay in their attitudinal ruts for long periods.

> **Norm.** Over two years ago, when he was passed over for a promotion he thought he deserved, Norm pushed himself into a negative rut. He is in the same trough today. Even if there were some easy way to tell Norm that he is negative, he would deny it because he has been in this entrenched rut so long that he thinks his behavior is normal. As a result, he cannot see he is his own worst enemy.

# Attitude and Stress

Job stress is self-imposed when workers set too many difficult goals for themselves and, as a result, move in an unorganized manner in too many directions at the same time. Most stress, however, is caused by the job itself. Some jobs—such as those of television news personnel, air traffic controllers, and police officers—are recognized as stressful.

Excessive stress can cause job burnout, which results in impairment of work productivity. Warning signals include feelings of frustration (Chapter 11), emotional outbursts, and withdrawal. Human relationships usually deteriorate.

*Do those who maintain positive attitudes handle stress better than others?*

Generally speaking, "yes." When you focus on the positive elements of a work environment, you are more apt to envision yourself as a winner. The result is that you laugh more and find it easier to relax. With these behavioral patterns, less stress affects the individual, and the stress that does occur is dissipated with less damage.

In contrast, those with behavioral patterns connected with negative attitudes appear to open the door to additional stress and hold the pressure created within themselves longer.

The more stress that can be removed from any job (fewer deadlines, unreasonable demands, human conflicts) the better. However, all jobs generate some stress. Whatever the stress level may be, those who concentrate on maintaining good co-worker relationships seem to handle it with less harm to themselves.

*Can returning to a positive from a negative attitude be considered an antidote to excessive stress and possible burnout?*

To a limited extent, "yes." When excessive stress eventually gets to workers, they often focus more on the negative factors present. After an attitude-renewal program takes place (vacation, counseling, self-help), these same people see the more positive factors present. In this sense, returning to their positive attitude constitutes an antidote.

The Attitude Adjustment Scale that follows is designed to help you assess the current condition of your own attitude. View it in the same manner you would one of those electronic instruments used to determine if your car engine needs a tune-up. The results might send you a signal that, with a few adjustments, you could be a more positive, successful, and happy person.

## ATTITUDE ADJUSTMENT SCALE

Use this exercise to rate your current attitude. Read each statement and circle the number where you feel you belong. If you circle a 10, you are saying your attitude could not be better in this area; if you circle a 1, you are saying it could not be worse.

|  | **High** **(Positive)** | **Low** **(Negative)** |
|---|---|---|
| 1. I'm not going to ask, but my honest guess is that my boss would now rate my general attitude as a . . . | 10 9 8 7 6 5 4 3 2 1 | |
| 2. Given a chance, co-workers and family would rate my attitude as a . . . | 10 9 8 7 6 5 4 3 2 1 | |
| 3. I would rate my attitude as a . . . | 10 9 8 7 6 5 4 3 2 1 | |
| 4. In dealing with others, I believe my current effectiveness rates a . . . | 10 9 8 7 6 5 4 3 2 1 | |
| 5. My current creativity level rates a . . . | 10 9 8 7 6 5 4 3 2 1 | |
| 6. If there were a meter to gauge my sense of humor at this stage, I believe it would read close to a . . . | 10 9 8 7 6 5 4 3 2 1 | |
| 7. My recent disposition—the patience and sensitivity I show to others—deserves a rating of . . . | 10 9 8 7 6 5 4 3 2 1 | |
| 8. For not letting little things bother me recently, I deserve a . . . | 10 9 8 7 6 5 4 3 2 1 | |
| 9. Based on the number of compliments I've received lately, I deserve a . . . | 10 9 8 7 6 5 4 3 2 1 | |
| 10. I would rate my enthusiasm toward my job and life in general during the past few weeks as a . . . | 10 9 8 7 6 5 4 3 2 1 | |

TOTAL _____

A score of 90 or over is a signal that your attitude is "in tune," and no adjustments are necessary; a score between 70 and 90 is a signal that minor adjustments may help; a score under 50 indicates that a complete overhaul may be required.

Regardless of how you rated yourself on the scale, the attitude-adjustment techniques that follow can help you become a more positive and effective individual.

## Adjustment 1: Employ the Flip-Side Technique

The pivotal factor between being positive or negative is often a sense of humor. Attitude and humor have a symbiotic relationship. The more you develop your sense of humor, the more positive you will become. The more positive you become, the better your sense of humor will be. It's a happy arrangement.

Some people successfully use the "flip-side technique" to maintain and enhance their sense of humor. When a "negative" enters their lives, they immediately flip the problem over (as you would a pancake) and look for whatever humor may exist on the other side. When they succeed, these clever individuals are able to minimize the negative impact the problem has on their positive attitude.

> **Jim.** When Jim walked into his apartment last night he was devastated. Everything was in shambles, and he quickly discovered that some valuable possessions were missing. After assessing the situation, Jim called Marcy and said; "I think I have figured out a way for us to take that vacation trip to Mexico. I've just been robbed, but my homeowners insurance is paid up. Why not come over and help me clean up while we finalize our plans?"

Humor in any form resists negative forces. It can restore your positive attitude and help you maintain a more balanced perspective on life.

How do you define a sense of humor?

A sense of humor is an attitudinal quality (mental focus) that encourages an individual to discover humor others may not see in the same situation. It is a philosophy that says: "If you take life too seriously, it will pull you down. Force yourself to pull back and laugh at the human predicament.

Countless incidents, which you could improve with a humorous twist, occur in your life each day. They will pass you by, however, unless you educate your attitude to see them. To find humor in a situation, it might be helpful for you to give this mental set a special name, such as *funny focus*. It may sound frivolous, but finding a funny focus describes what some wise people are actually able to do.

"Susan always adjusts more quickly because she directs that creative mind of hers to the funny side."

"Sam is good company because he has the unique capacity to find humor in any situation."

Those who receive such compliments nurture a funny focus that permits them to create a more positive perspective. A humorous focus is their antidote to negative situations.

How can you improve your attitude through a greater sense of humor? How can you develop a funny focus that will fall within your comfort zone? Recognizing the following elements should help.

■ *Humor is an inside job.* Humor is not something that is natural for one person and unnatural for another. One individual is not blessed with a reservoir of humor waiting to be released, while another is left to cry. A sense of humor is created. With practice, anyone can do it.

■ *Laughter is therapeutic.* Negative emotions such as tension, anger, or stress can produce ulcers, headaches, and high blood pressure. Positive emotions can relax nerves, improve digestion and circulation, and otherwise contribute to physical and emotional wellness. Of course, you can't laugh away all serious problems, but you can laugh your way into a more positive focus to help you cope with the problem. Laughter is soul music to attitude. It is a way of adjusting to a funny focus.

■ A *funny focus can get you out of the problem and into the solution.* Finding the humor in a situation usually won't solve a problem, but it can lead you in the right direction. Laughing can help transfer your focus from the problem to the solution. Using the flip-side technique starts the process.

## Adjustment 2: Play Your Winners

When retailers discover that a certain item is selling faster than others, they pour additional promotional money into that product. Their motto is. "Play the winners; don't go broke trying to promote the losers."

The same approach can help you adjust and maintain a positive attitude. You have special winners in your life. *The more you focus on them, the better.*

**Jason.** At this point in his life, Jason has more losers than winners. Having spent ten years in the work force, he is currently adjusting to a divorce, is deeply in debt, and has a car that is giving him fits. The only two positive factors are his job (Jason is making progress in the hotel management field he loves) and running. By pouring his energies into his career and running a minimum of six miles each day, Jason is able to maintain a positive attitude. He is playing his winners.

Each of us, at any stage in our lives, is confronted with both positive factors (winners) and negative factors (losers). If you are not constantly alert, losers can take over and push your winners out of your mental focus. When winners get shoved to the sidelines, you spend mind time dwelling on your losers. If continued over a period of time, your attitude will become negative and your disposition will turn sour. *Your challenge is to find ways to push the losers to the perimeter of your thinking,* where you can live with them, per-haps permanently, in a graceful manner.

How can you do this?

Here are three simple suggestions:

1. *THINK more about your winners.* The more you concentrate on the win-ning elements in your life, the less time you will have to devote to the negatives. Thinking about winners means that your negative factors will receive less attention and, as a result, many may resolve themselves.

2. *TALK only about your winners.* As long as you don't overdo it (or repeat yourself with the same person), the more you verbalize the happy, ex-citing factors in your life, the more important they become to you. Those who talk incessantly about the negative aspects of their lives do their friends a disservice and perpetuate their own negative attitude.

3. *REWARD yourself by enjoying your winners.* If you enjoy nature, play this winner by taking a nature walk. If music is a positive influence, listen to your favorite artist. If religion is a powerful force in your life, play your winner by praying.

You play your winners every time you think or talk or pray about them. But obviously, the best thing you can do is *enjoy* them. If you are a golfer, playing eighteen holes will do more for your attitude than thinking or talk-ing about doing it.

## Adjustment 3: Give Your Positive Attitude to Others

When you get fed up with the behavior of others, you may be tempted to tell them off and give them "a piece of your mind." Telling someone off is understandably human. It is a better policy, however, to give others "a piece of your positive attitude." When you react positively, you permit others to help you adjust your attitude.

> **Shannon.** Because she needed a psychological lift, Shannon asked Casey to meet her for lunch. Casey didn't feel much like it, but she accepted and made a special effort to be upbeat. When the luncheon was over, Casey had not only given Shannon a boost, she felt better herself. Both women came out ahead.

When you give part of your positive attitude to others, you create a sym-biotic relationship. The recipient feels better, but so do you. In a somewhat upside-down twist, *you keep your positive attitude by giving it away.*

Everyone has opportunities to give their positive attitudes to others. Taxi drivers who make their passengers laugh will increase their tips; employees who give co-workers deserved compliments increase their popularity; homeowners who send positive signals to neighbors thus eliminate problems with them when they see them; and vacationers can enhance their fun by making new friends simply by being pleasant to fellow travelers. Opportunities abound. The results are best, however, when the giving is toughest.

> **Enid.** It was a difficult Friday for Enid. Due to an emergency staff meeting in the morning, she was behind in her work. Just as she was starting to catch up, the computer went down. Then her boss asked her to finish an unexpected project before leaving for the weekend. When she finally left work, all Enid could think of was getting into her jacuzzi and forgetting it all. But she had promised herself to visit her friend Wanda, who was hospitalized. The temptation to drive straight home was strong, but she resisted and paid Wanda a visit. An hour later, Enid arrived home refreshed and positive. She didn't need the jacuzzi.

Each individual winds up a winner by giving his (or her) positive attitude away in a manner suited to his own personal style.

## Adjustment 4: Look Better to Yourself

You are constantly bombarded through media advertising to improve your image. Most messages state that only with a "new look" can you find acceptance and meet new friends.

"Discover the new you. Join our health club and expand your circle of friends."

"Let cosmetic surgery help you find a new partner."

Self-improvement of any kind should be applauded. However, the overriding reason for a "new image" is not to look better for others, but for yourself. When you improve your appearance, you give your positive attitude a boost. It is not what happens outside that counts, but how your mind sees yourself.

While the term *inferiority complex* is not in popular use today, the old textbook definition is a good one: *An inferiority complex is said to occur when you look better to others than you do to yourself.* In other words, when you have a negative self-image, you *make* yourself feel psychologically inferior when you probably are not.

The truth is that you often do look better to others than to yourself. There may be periods when you feel unfashionable, unattractive, and dowdy—but this does not mean you look that way to your friends. The problem is that you are communicating a negative attitude because you don't look good to yourself.

When you have a poor self-image, it is as though you are looking through a glass darkly. You feel you don't look good, so nothing else looks good to you. Getting down on yourself occurs because your negative image psychologically distorts your attitude (the way you look at things mentally).

You see yourself first, your environment second. You can't remove yourself from the perceptual process.

**Luis.**    When he was a teenager, Luis gave up on ever having a good self-image. All through college he was considered a reclusive grind. Approaching graduation, Luis enrolled in a noncredit course designed to prepare students for a professional job search. Part of the program included doing a mock employment interview on videotape that would be critiqued by the instructor and fellow students. To prepare for this unwanted ordeal, Luis purchased a new suit, had his hair restyled, and bought new, more fashionable eye glass frames. He practiced his mock interview over and over at home. When his day arrived, Luis did so well that he received compliments from all who viewed the tape. The recognition and support had a wonderful impact on Luis. For the first time, he looked good to himself. Luis's negative image was no longer a barrier to a good future.

The connection between a good self-image and a positive attitude cannot be ignored. In keeping a better image, it will help if you

- admit that at times you may look better to others than you look to yourself;

- play up your winning features—hair, smile, eyes, etc.; and

- make improvements in grooming—when improvement is possible.

## Adjustment 5: Accept the Physical Connection

Apparently no one has been able to prove conclusively that there is a direct relationship between physical well-being and attitude. Most, however, including the most cynical researchers in the area, concede that there is a connection.

More than any previous generation, today's young adults are aware of physical fitness. A surprising number incorporate daily workouts into their schedules. Their commitment to the "attitude connection" is expressed in these typical comments:

"My workout does as much for my attitude as it does for my body."

"Exercise tones up my body and tunes up my outlook."

"I never underestimate what working out does for me psychologically."

Many fitness enthusiasts depend upon exercise to keep them out of attitudinal ruts:

"I've renamed my health club 'The Attitude Adjustment Factory.'"

"I take a long walk to push negative thoughts out of my system."

"An unusually tough workout will often get me out of a mental rut."

No single group in our society gives such full attention to the psychological aspects of attitude than professional athletes. Increasingly, athletes engage year round in sophisticated physical conditioning programs. They realize they must stay in shape to remain competitive.

"Our same football team finished in the cellar last year. We made the play-offs this year because we have a new team attitude."

"I owe my success this season to my wife. She helped me adjust my attitude."

"My success this year is 90 percent due to a better attitude."

They must be trying to tell us something.

> *Frequent attitude renewal can turn ruts and roadblocks into unforeseen opportunities.*

## Case 23

**"I'll adjust later."**

# Focus

Up until about a year ago, Cathy made monthly deposits to her savings account. When shortly thereafter she took a higher paying job, Cathy was sure she could get back to saving again. But, instead, she has continued to "dip" into her savings and is now using these funds to pay for her maxed out credit cards. She is facing serious debt. Just last week, her boss told her that her positive attitude has slipped, her interaction with fellow employees is deteriorating, and she seems disinterested in her work. Furthermore, her tardiness (as a result of her "quick" shopping trips to the nearby mall) is chronic. If she doesn't get back on track, she may lose her job. Shopping is what gives Cathy a boost—isn't it? At least she thought it did until she really stopped to analyze it. Has she lost focus?

Lupe is suffering from the "campus blahs." With finals only a few weeks away, Lupe has lost her motivation to excel. Everything is a drag. Could it be excessive study time? A demanding part-time job? Home problems? Whatever the reason, she is even discouraged about her personal image. Why must life be so out of focus?

Arnold appears to be approaching career burnout. A very hardworking, highly successful professional sales representative, Arnold senses that he has lost touch with customers. For the first time, they are reacting negatively to his approach. Despite his need for more money to cover new personal financial commitments, his commission check last month was lower than in previous months. Even his daily jogging is not helping him maintain a positive attitude. Why are things so out of focus?

Would you recommend the five adjustment techniques to Cathy, Lupe, and Arnold? Which do you think would help Cathy the most? Lupe? Arnold? Why? (For a suggested answer, see page 234.)

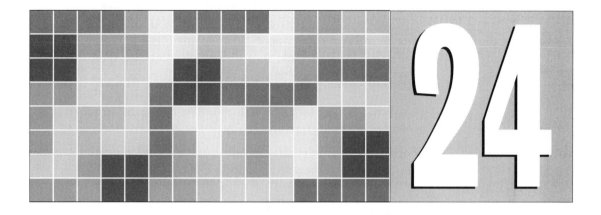

# Moving Up to Leadership/ Management

**"Being a supervisor can be a big headache."**

Thought for the Day: Because living is the pursuit of learning over a lifetime, always strive to become the best you can be.

By improving your human-relations skills and achieving greater insight into your positive attitude, you possess the foundation upon which you can build a more promising career. Such a career may lead you into business management or a leadership role in a different career area of your choice. Two things are certain:

- *The more you practice sound human relations as an employee, the more likely it is that your superiors will promote you into management.*

- *Everything you learn and practice about attitude and good human relations now will help you achieve a leadership position later.*

## Dual Competency

Wherever you may be employed now or in the future, your superiors will probably be sensitive to the fact that you are building and maintaining better relationships with people than your co-workers and that you know how to operate effectively in a group—that you have a double competency. You are skillful technically. You are also skillful with people. Observing this double competency, your superiors will naturally assume that if you are good at human relations at the employee level, you will also be good at the management level. It is a wise assumption. Let's look at what happened to Cleo.

> **Cleo.**  A highly competent computer technician, Cleo concentrated on her personal productivity, but she did not neglect her human-relations skills. She would frequently stop her own work to help someone with a problem. She would sometimes pitch in at the end of the day to help others get out an urgent report. Her efforts to help her co-workers did not go unrecognized.
>
> Cleo was invited to attend a supervisory course on company time. Two weeks after the course was over, she became a supervisor. She was elated, not only because she had very little seniority, but also because she was the youngest person in her department. Her quick promotion made her respect her human-relations skills more than ever.

## Self-Confidence

The best thing about becoming more human-relations competent is that it makes one more self-confident. It happens every time. In short, the more you practice the human-relations skills discussed in this book, the more self-confidence you will build. Learning to establish strong working relationships with those who are older and more experienced than you is confidence building. Being able to restore a damaged relationship is confidence building. The more you can prove to yourself that you are good at people skills, the less likely it is that you will be intimidated by others. Soon you will discover that you can work effectively with sophisticated, experienced superiors at all levels; soon you will feel sufficiently confident to step out in front and be a leader. Jerry is a good case in point.

> **Jerry.** A sensitive and quiet young man, Jerry completed a self-study course in human relations because he wanted to develop more meaningful relationships with people both on and off the job. It was a personal goal of Jerry's. He had no thoughts of ever becoming a leader. Such a role, he thought, was beyond his capacity. Yet within two years, Jerry was so good at building relationships with co-workers that his personal confidence had increased significantly. To both management and fellow workers, he became a different person. When he was asked to become a supervisor, the only one surprised was Jerry himself.

## Sensitivity

When you demonstrate the self-confidence that practicing good human relations produces, new career doors automatically open. You may or may not choose to enter such doors, but it will be personally rewarding to know they are open.

Your transition into a supervisory role should be smooth because all the human-relations competencies you practice as an employee can be transferred to your new role. In fact, some skills will make more sense to you as a supervisor. For example, having tried, perhaps unsuccessfully, to build a relationship with a difficult supervisor, you will be more sensitive to the problem once you are there yourself. Knowing how a conflict between two co-workers can injure the productivity of all, you will pick up on such situations faster and intervene sooner. Knowing the rewards your supervisor could have given you but didn't, you will be more sensitive to your employees' need for recognition. This is what happened to Geraldine.

> **Geraldine.** Disturbed by the behavior and insensitivity of her supervisor, Geraldine swore she would never become one herself. Then, because of a dramatic change in her personal life, she had second thoughts. Her rationale was as follows: because the managers in my field are so ineffective, the opportunities should be limitless for someone like me who is willing to learn how to be a good supervisor.
>
> What did Geraldine do? She took a basic course in human-relations skills and another course in management. As she studied, she made mental notes of the skills she would employ that her present manager did not. Her management opportunity came sooner than she anticipated; and because of her basic preparation, the transition was smooth. Geraldine has since received two additional promotions. What she learned as an employee provided her with a ticket to career success.

# What About You?

Should you pursue a management role? If you are already in a supervisory role, should you strike out for something in middle or upper management? The decision, of course, deserves careful consideration. Here are some thoughts you might wish to ponder.

■ *Accept the edge you already possess, but admit you have much to learn.*

Many capable supervisors study human relations after they get their jobs. Many also admit they started out with a handicap because they did not have a strong enough human-relations background. Keep in mind that human relations is not the only thing a supervisor must know. There are many special supervisory skills that must be learned. Learning how to delegate, to conduct formal appraisals, to set priorities, to make decisions, and to manage one's time are critical supervisory skills.* If you wish to succeed in a management role, it will be necessary for you to become competent in these areas. You may wish to study these skills in anticipation of your first supervisory role.

■ *Management training is increasingly demanding.*

Even if you prepare for and become an excellent supervisor, it is only a start. The more you may aspire to upper-management roles, the more training you should receive. The master of business administration (MBA) graduate degree has become the standard goal of many. Earning a MBA means taking demanding courses in statistics, computer science, information technology, management theory, finance, and other areas. If you decide to take this route to the top, keep in mind that in most cases you can earn a MBA while working full time.

■ *If you are intrigued with human relations, it is probably a sign that you will also like management.*

Although there are many facets to a management job, most involve considerable interaction with people. A management job involves counseling, leadership development, and building a competent staff. Some corporate presidents devote over 80 percent of their time to people problems. It is true that an executive manages resources and capital, but the first priority is working with people. The need to work with people will not change.

---

*Also available from this publisher is Chapman/Goodwin, *Supervisor's Survival Kit*, 9th ed., 2001, Prentice Hall, Upper Saddle River, New Jersey 07458.

- *The discipline factor may not be for you.*

Those who are not in supervisory roles have the luxury of building re-warding relationships without having to assume the responsibility of cor-recting the behavior of others. Human relations at the worker level does not involve discipline. Some individuals who are outstanding at human rela-tions are so sensitive to the needs of others and so compassionate in their association with others that they cannot correct or discipline those who get out of line. These people are uncomfortable in most leadership roles. They should, therefore, remain workers and make their contribution at that level. Not only will they be unhappy with the constant responsibility to disci-pline, they probably will not do it well.

- *Could you make hard decisions?*

Supervisors must make many decisions each day. The further up the ex-ecutive ladder a supervisor goes, the more critical the decisions become. Most decisions are people decisions and, frequently, people decisions are very difficult ones to make. And even those that are primarily productivity or financial decisions affect people.

The fact that you are good at human relations does not necessarily mean that you will be good at decision making. Indeed, the opposite may be true. For example, a manager may have to make a decision to give a layoff notice to a loyal and competent employee—perhaps even one with whom the man-ager has an outstanding relationship. There is some indication that the bet-ter you are at human relations, the more traumatic such a decision can be. No doubt, you will want to weigh the decision-making factor carefully be-fore deciding to become a supervisor or manager.

- *Management people are more vulnerable.*

If you are a highly sensitive person (one reason why you may be good at building positive relationships with others), you may find it difficult to accept the criticism that goes along with a management role. Few, if any, managers are without detractors. In fact, whether or not a leader remains a leader, often depends upon keeping detractors at a minimum or spotting them soon enough to bring them into the fold.

Do not misunderstand. Your human-relations skills will help you to build good relationships with employees and thus minimize the possibility of negative reactions. You may never have someone under your supervision who becomes so disenchanted that she (or he) sets out to get you. But the possibility exists. Despite your own abilities, the role itself makes you more vulnerable. Knowing that a supervisor or manager is more vulnerable to negative human-relations problems is in no way intended to keep you from wanting to become a supervisor; it simply means that there are disadvantages you should consider in advance.

- *Your personal attitude is more important in a management role—not less!*

As a supervisor, maintaining your own positive attitude—staying out of attitudinal ruts—is critical. A negative attitude in front of employees is a luxury a person in management cannot afford.

Successful supervisors and leaders at all levels have the ability to create a positive force that pulls employees into a circle of involvement and activity. Once this force gets started, it seems to generate confidence among all team members and leads to constructive action and higher productivity.

How do you create a positive force?

Like a pebble dropped into a quiet pool, the power of your positive attitude gets things started. Thus, as a leader, your positive attitude is the source of your power. Your positive attitude communicates to those being led that they are headed in a direction that will eventually provide benefits. There are exciting goals within reach. Something better lies over the horizon. A positive attitude in a supervisor/leader builds positive expectations in the minds of workers, whereas a negative attitude destroys them.

## Management/Leadership Challenge

The management/leadership challenge is, for many, exciting and rewarding. Those who have taken a leadership career path claim that the challenge has forced them to recognize that their positive attitudes are, indeed, priceless possessions.

Now that you have achieved new insights into human behavior and the importance of your own attitude, you are in a better position to decide whether management or leadership roles are for you.

Good luck! And always keep in mind that *your attitude is showing!*

> *If you could assume the attitude*
> *of your choice, is YOURS the*
> *one you would select?*

# Case 24

**"I'm chained to my present role."**

# Sensitivity

Bernice is, without question, the most popular and respected employee in her division. She has the rare talent of being able to build meaningful relationships quickly, but she is even better at maintaining them. Her sensitivity to the needs of others is amazing. Co-workers come to her for help on both work-oriented and personal problems, and she seems to have sufficient patience to handle them all.

One fellow employee, however, puts it this way: "Bernice is a pleasure to know and to work with. I sometimes wish she was our supervisor, but I'm afraid the job would chew her up. She is just too nice. It would be difficult, perhaps impossible, for her to get tough and set a firm discipline line. And problem employees would worry her to death."

Recently, management invited Bernice to become a supervisor of one of the departments in the division. Management believes she is so well liked by co-workers that she obviously has leadership potential.

Assume that you are a close friend. Would you recommend that Bernice accept the invitation? (For a suggested answer, see page 235.)

# Suggested Answers to Cases

The human-relations cases presented at the end of each chapter in this book are designed to be springboards for individual thinking and discussion purposes. There are no exact answers to any of the cases.

In the first place, only the most essential facts of each case are outlined. It is therefore impossible to give definite or complete answers to any case. Without all the facts, anything approaching a definite or complete answer would be dangerous indeed. Also, different points of view are always possible (even encouraged) in discussions of human-relations cases.

The following so-called answers, then, are nothing more than an account of how we would approach the case with the available facts. They should serve only as a guide to the independent thinking of the reader and the discussion leader.

## Case 1: Reality

It is easy to understand why Rod was disturbed when the other two received promotions ahead of him. His pride was hurt because he had worked hard and efficiently at his job. But there is at least some evidence that Rod was trying to escape his full human-relations responsibility. Did he make enough effort to cooperate and build good relationships with his co-workers, or did he put everything into personal productivity?

The authors believe that Rod was not fully justified in saying, "It isn't what you know, but who you know that counts." It appears that Rod was trying to rationalize his unwillingness to build better relationships. He was reminded twice by his supervisor to be more a part of the group. He did not take the advice.

He did not see why he had more of a responsibility to work closely with others in his department in order to help their productivity. Rod's supervisor might have counseled him sooner, more often, and in a more sensitive manner. The supervisor might have given Rod both good and bad examples from the behavior of others. Rod appears to need feedback about the specific negative behaviors he demonstrates, the impact they have on others, and some suggested alternatives. The supervisor must assume some of the responsibility for Rod's poor human-relations performance.

Rod's case shows that an ambitious employee who works hard and efficiently does not necessarily make career progress. Rod needs to develop a better balance between productivity and human-relations skills to reach his potential.

## Case 2: Adjustment

It would appear that George must learn to relax and give more of himself if he wants to find an environment in which he can be happy and productive. He will never make his maximum contribution to his job and his company if he stays deep inside his shell and expects others to come to him.

George would probably have to make some concessions before he finds another job where he would be happy. He failed to understand that when he was aloof and distant, he made it uncomfortable for others. He failed to comprehend that his fellow workers might have needed to communicate with him on a friendly basis whether or not he needed to communicate with them.

In discussing the matter with George, his supervisor might try to increase George's confidence to reach out and communicate more with others. George does not yet fully sense why he should communicate more. Thus (using specific examples that George would appreciate), stress could be placed on why it is difficult to work next to a poor communicator. That is, people who act aloof or distant have a way of irritating others. It could also be pointed out that such behavior is often misinterpreted—a negative or avoidance response from a person with whom you try to become friendly can cause you to withdraw. The supervisor's success with George would depend, in part, upon the supervisor's skill in getting George to talk more while the supervisor talks less and listens more effectively.

## Case 3: Credit Blues

Although some people can control their consumer credit financing patterns, others seem to get in over their heads. They soon struggle to keep up with the interest charges on their statements in addition to making payments on principal amounts. When this occurs, a drastic cutback in living standards is often dictated. Only a few people seem to go through such an experience without its having a negative impact on their attitude. Their academic goals and careers are often permanently derailed.

Since it appears Manuel is facing serious financial problems, some suggestions for him include the following:

1. Curtail consumer spending immediately. If necessary, Manuel should destroy his credit cards.

2. Seek less expensive forms of recreation.

3. Accept financial guidance from an expert.

4. Prepare and follow a monthly budget.

5. Anticipate a slow recovery.

Once Manuel is able to see the light at the end of his financial tunnel, his boss and co-workers will probably notice an improvement in his attitude, and his career will be back on track. Manuel might have learned that his positive attitude could be his most priceless possession.

## Case 4: Bounce Back

Counseling a highly sensitive individual on any facet of attitude is a difficult challenge. That Frank is a male nurse shouldn't make it more difficult, but the fact that Frank is one of her supervisors and an authority figure might. Frank will need all of his counseling skills. Once Sue Ellen relaxes and senses that Frank really wants to help, progress is a possibility. Frank should try to reach these goals: (1) Convince Sue Ellen that there is probably nothing personal about people stepping on her attitude—it is simply a characteristic of the work environment. Patients can be unreasonable. Doctors, under pressure, also can be unreasonable. She should endeavor to not take such verbal abuse personally. (2) Illustrate that everyone gets their attitudes stepped on and everyone must learn how to cope with it in their own way. Sue Ellen needs to know that she is not being singled out. (3) Assure her that with effort, her personal confidence will increase; and encourage her to make a goal out of whipping the problem. Frank may want to make it a goal between the two of them so Frank can compliment her on the progress she shows. With the reinforcement Frank provides in this manner, Sue Ellen will become a stronger person and will have a brighter career future.

## Case 5: Decision

It is a smart strategy for Bernie to concentrate on building good horizontal relationships—but not to the point where he ignores any opportunity to build a relationship with Gloria, his aloof boss. Even though Gloria may appear to be unapproachable, Bernie should continue to wait and watch for opportunities to build a stronger relationship through hard work, friendliness, suggestions for improvements, and other means. Just because others have failed to build a healthy relationship with the supervisor doesn't mean that Bernie should give up. He could easily make the mistake of putting all of his human-relations eggs in one horizontal basket.

## Case 6: Message

The decision to pass Jeff over for the supervisory position is a good one for the following reasons:

1. It would be natural for Jeff's co-workers to resent him as a supervisor. He failed to build good horizontal working relationships with them when he had the chance. Productivity, under his leadership, could drop substantially.

2. An individual who doesn't learn how to build good horizontal relationships as an employee will probably have trouble building good vertical relationships as a supervisor. By neglecting his horizontal working relationships when he first joined the department, Jeff made a classic human-relations mistake.

3. A supervisor achieves more departmental productivity by building good relationships than from the work he actually performs. Jeff would be a poor risk as a supervisor.

Jeff's supervisor should have counseled him more and pointed out other examples of how high producers were passed over at promotion time. He should have explained the relationship between human relations and productivity when he first recognized that Jeff had a problem; that might have enabled Jeff to understand the "big picture." Jeff would thus have had a fair chance to correct his human-relations problem and ready himself for the next supervisory position opportunity.

## Case 7: Insight

Ted's impatience and exasperation are understandable. But the supervisor had a point and was right in counseling him to keep his cool and not further damage his horizontal relationships. Ted was well along the way to becoming a supervisor. If he had continued being critical of others, he might have forfeited his opportunity.

It should be pointed out, however, that Ted was in a tough spot. Due to jealousy and other conflict-causing human factors, it is a human-relations challenge to maintain a personal productivity level above that of your co-workers and still maintain good relations with them. However, if

Ted really wanted to be the next supervisor, this was the price he might have to pay.

The supervisor was wrong in not giving Ted the "human-relations story" before he became frustrated and damaged his horizontal relationships. Ted must learn, however, that few supervisors are perfect, and that he must protect his future by being human-relations sensitive even when his supervisor is not.

## Case 8: Choice

You have a difficult choice. The older, Theory X supervisor might give you the following advantages: (1) he has been with the company longer and has had more experience, so he might be able to teach you more; and (2) although he may demand more from you, in the long run you might be a stronger person and eventually a better supervisor yourself because of it.

If you choose the younger, Theory Y supervisor, you might enjoy the following advantages: (1) you would probably become more involved under her leadership and, as a result, more productive; and (2) this supervisor would probably move up the management ladder sooner. If you work hard, you might be able to take her place and move even higher later on because of her influence from above.

In answering the problem, consider the following:

1. In which work environment would you be most motivated and productive?

2. How would your personality and your values work with each supervisor?

3. How ambitious are you to get into management?

If you fully understand the leadership styles of each of the two supervisors, you should be able to make the best decision. If you are adaptable, though, neither environment should hurt your personal progress.

## Case 9: Currency

When money is the only currency one finds important, in the long run he (or she) is apt to be shortchanged. The authors would side with Ralph and build a case in the discussion that those who select careers in harmony with their values often come out ahead financially, too, because they build stronger human ties and remain more positive. Those who stay true to their values often enhance their leadership qualities (they gain more respect from followers) and, as a result, qualify for higher-paying positions. There is no documented evidence that those who deal only in the currency of money wind up with more of it.

# Case 10: Controversy

It is easy to justify the comments of both Justine and Zeke. Although it may sound simplistic for Justine to say that "if we treated everyone as an individual" life would be better for everyone, it remains a sound principle of good human relations. Zeke, of course, has a point in saying that people need to be rated on their performances in the work environment and on their value as human beings in society as a whole. Taking sides becomes a tricky and complicated part of the conversation. A combination of both views is probably the elegant response.

# Case 11: Frustration

A divorce can be a devastating event in one's life. Many other personal things also can affect one's overall behavior; however, Allen needs to get a grip on his frustration and aggressive behavior. He needs to consider how negative his attitude has become and how it is affecting him and everyone around him. He can't continue to blame everything on his personal life—and chastise others for it. He appears to be looking for ways to alienate people. His lashing out at work, at home, and even in public against people he doesn't even know suggests he has very deep-seated anger. Suggestions for improving his attitude include doing some physical exercise where he can get physically tired and find a release for his negative energy. He should consider directing his aggression to tennis or swimming, to yard work or house cleaning, or to similar activities as a diversion. He must find some positive ways to rebuild his life—to stop his self-pity. It's not going to be an easy road for Allen, and maybe some professional help is needed; but unless he takes action to turn his behavior around, he faces considerable more risk—possibly losing his job, alienating his children, becoming a loner, and being nothing but miserable.

# Case 12: Restoration

The chances of a full restoration are slim, but the luncheon meeting stands a good chance of pushing the conflict underground so it will not be so obvious to other workers. In other words, both Doreen and Crystal may learn to have more respect for each other and work together on a higher human-relations level than in the past.

Also if Mrs. Ruby does not have a good possibility for a transfer option, she should not suggest such an option. Her transfer suggestion could make both supervisors resentful of her and the conflict then becomes a three-way conflict.

## Case 13: Communication

Jack may want to take the long view and find his best solution by communicating freely and openly with his family, especially his wife. There is the strong possibility that Jack can slowly build a mutually rewarding relationship with Yoshio. For example, Yoshio could reward Jack by giving him more responsibility and authority, while Jack could reward Yoshio by helping him improve his communication skills. With this exchange, Jack might eventually earn a promotion or an even better job in the same organization. . . . All of this without removing his family from their present comfort zone.

The big danger for Jack is that he might permit the new situation (Yoshio getting the job Jack wanted) to turn him negative on a permanent basis. This often happens.

## Case 14: Nonprofessional

Helen is in a delicate position. The behavior of Thomas in apparently plagiarizing Helen's ideas would be considered unprofessional, if not unethical, by most people. But, if she blows the whistle on Thomas without written proof, her accusation could be interpreted by management as "sour grapes" and her own image could be damaged. Although Helen might be tempted to confront Thomas with the matter in front of others, she should resist. Confronting Thomas could irritate and embarrass him, causing him to go behind her back and perhaps hurt Helen even more at a later date. It could also make Helen look bad to co-workers. Helen could, however, confront Thomas in private, so that he knows what he will be up against in the future. She could also protect her creative ideas in the future by refusing to discuss them informally in advance and by submitting them in writing after they have been fully developed.

Openness is a vital part of human relations. Devious co-workers often destroy the element of trust that is vital in any long-term relationship. The reader is encouraged to isolate and learn from other examples of nonprofessional behavior.

## Case 15: Confrontation

John did the right thing under the circumstances. After two months, he had had sufficient time to discover that the cause of Ms. Robertson's critical attitude was deep-seated and that time alone would probably not solve the problem. John took time to investigate and gather some facts. He discovered, among other things, that two former employees in his position resigned because of Ms. Robertson and her attitude. In other words, this was not surface teasing or testing.

Although John took a serious human-relations risk by standing up to Ms. Robertson, he had at least a fair chance of resolving the problem and helping his future. If he was successful, everybody would come out ahead, including the company and Ms. Robertson.

The reader may not fully agree with the way John approached Ms. Robertson or the way in which he expressed himself. To some it may appear that he was too direct and forceful. To others he may have appeared to be overly apologetic. Everyone must go about confrontations of this nature in his (or her) own individual manner. But the principle remains that the cards must often be laid on the table if a sound working relationship is to be created or restored.

As a supervisor in a similar situation, the supervisor should initiate a three-way discussion to air differences openly. The supervisor could then introduce the MRT concept and suggest that Ms. Robertson and John try to find a few mutual rewards that might help them build a positive relationship. Lastly, the supervisor should follow through by complimenting both employees on any progress made, in the hope that such recognition would encourage them to continue to make a strong effort to build a sound relationship.

# Case 16: Balance

Lorraine's absenteeism is getting out of hand and could be called chronic. Her firm could make a reasonable effort to help her learn how to do a better job of balancing home and career. Learning the proper balance could be accomplished through a series of discussions or in a seminar focused on the importance of attendance. Lorraine needs to see the negative impact of her sporadic absenteeism upon company productivity and co-worker relationships. Once this has been achieved, it would be advisable for Lorraine to identify what she can do to reduce her absenteeism.

When an employee "owns" the problem, he (or she) must do the problem solving. Accepting problem ownership will preserve self-esteem and maintain a healthy manager/employee relationship. With such an attitude, Lorraine and Mr. Hodges should have no trouble working out an action plan that everyone can live with as the problem is addressed. They also need to agree on a time period that will allow Lorraine to bring her absenteeism under control. To start with, she must begin by calling in to Mr. Hodges each and every time she needs to be absent. Being certain that she is truthful every time she gives a reason for her absence will also help Lorraine build both her credibility and her self-discipline, presuming that she values her job and wishes to remain employed there.

If such efforts do not bring positive results, the firm would be justified in starting termination procedures according to personnel policy and legal restrictions. One employee cannot be permitted to drag down the productivity over an extended period of time. Lorraine, of all people, should appreciate the need for following procedures—she works with policies and procedures whenever she is on the job!

## Case 17: Motivation

Barry seems to be out of tune with the modern, high-tempo workplace. He seems to be operating on the ultra-simplistic premise that management has the sole responsibility to motivate employees. Perhaps this comes from Barry's past, where he leaned too heavily on his parents, teachers, and mentors for motivation.

First, Barry must be willing to *listen* to his supervisor and other seasoned employees while learning not to underestimate them. They apparently have Barry's best interests at heart and want him to succeed. He will need also to consider the principle of openly admitting his mistake (that he "may not have been trying as hard as he could") to his supervisor. Since he is a new employee, his supervisor will most likely give Barry another chance to perform at his competence level. On his own, Barry also needs to start associating with some ambitious co-workers who are scrambling for better roles and greater effectiveness in the workplace. He will soon discover the depth of their self-motivation and will decide whether he is interested in applying his exceptional skills and competencies to become competitive and demonstrate commitment to his job and the organization.

## Case 18: Dilemma

Sylvia made two mistakes. First, she accepted as fact a comment that was not authenticated and could easily have been a rumor. Her second mistake was more serious: she permitted the possible rumor to disturb her emotionally, to the point where it noticeably hurt her productivity.

The facts were not presented in the case, but it is quite possible that the real reason Mr. Young was made department head instead of Sylvia was that Sylvia's efficiency on the job had dropped to the point where management decided to pass her over. If this was what happened, Sylvia permitted a simple rumor to do the greatest possible damage to her future.

## Case 19: Conflict

Goal-oriented people usually want to get on with their lives and may run out of patience waiting for those who are still searching. A marriage seems to work best when both partners are goal oriented and have some strong common goals they are trying to reach. It would appear that it is best for Deric and RayLyn to go their separate ways at this juncture. If, in a few years, they discover that their love for each other has been sufficiently strong to hold up during periods of separation, their relationship could be restored.

# Case 20: Preference

Angelo has an intriguing but difficult decision ahead of him. In making it, he should take a long look at himself and the direction he desires his career path to take. How important is immediate monetary success versus long-range security to him? What are his long-term goals? If Angelo becomes impatient and frustrated over slow but steady progress, he should think twice about joining a company that has modest growth potential and makes a practice of promoting from within. The zigzag route to the top might be best.

On the other hand, if Angelo is comfortable with slower but more secure growth, Company B may be his better choice. Company B may provide more and better training, will perhaps encourage him to get an advanced college degree in management at its expense, and will offer a more comprehensive benefit package. Of course, all of this depends upon the future stability of the company. Even firms with strong PFW policies must sometimes go through reorganizations, consolidations, and layoffs.

If Angelo is seeking more immediate upward mobility and is willing to take the higher risks involved, Company A may be his best choice. Company A may push more responsibility his way sooner. He should keep in mind that he may have to get more training, and there is always the possibility that he may need to scramble to another company.

# Case 21: Change

Both Ingrid and Darla may be successful in adjusting to the dynamic changes of the future, but Darla appears to be more realistic. When change occurs in most organizations, it is not business as usual and most employees can benefit from a new approach.

Darla is to be applauded for her philosophy of trying to turn change into opportunity, but "looking out for number one" often has a devious connotation that implies a departure from normal ethical and sound human-relations principles to get ahead. If deviousness is Darla's strategy, her efforts could prove to be counterproductive because she could injure relationships that might provide support she could need at a later date.

Perhaps a combination of maintaining high productivity and sound human relations (Ingrid) with a creative approach to turning change into opportunity (Darla) is the best approach. It should also be added that education is the best possible preparation for adapting to change.

# Case 22: Interview

The following answers can be considered models:

1. "In doing my pre-interview investigation, I discovered that you have an ambitious expansion program and that you have an excellent reputation within the industry for treating people fairly. These features appeal to me."

2. "I will bring my present professional sales skills with me—I feel competent in organizing client data, in my ability to close sales, and about handling rejection—and I would develop other skills such as handling objections on your product line. My goal would be to reach a role where my leadership would help build a stronger organization through teamwork and a balanced emphasis on productivity and sales."

3. "I have concentrated on developing my human-relations competencies. I can build good relationships with co-workers and superiors. When I make a mistake, I can repair a relationship. I have received compliments for my skills in problem solving. I am also sensitive to the needs of others. I am a good listener. I understand the positive associations between high productivity and good human relations—especially where clients are concerned."

4. "I have trouble maintaining my enthusiasm over a long period of time, and I tend to scatter my energy in too many directions. I'm working to make improvements in both areas." (NOTE: Giving more specifics on how you are turning your weaknesses into strengths will focus you and the interviewer on your positive vs. negative attributes.)

# Case 23: Focus

All of the adjustment techniques could help Cathy, Lupe, and Arnold, provided they first *recognize* that they are in an attitudinal rut and need a major renewal program. Cathy might benefit most from exchanging her shopping (which is not satisfying her) for a workout or physical training routine (Adjustment 5) as well as placing more emphasis on her winners (Adjustment 2). Lupe might benefit most from revitalizing her attitude by giving it away to others (Adjustment 3) and looking better to herself (Adjustment 4). Arnold might benefit most from the flip-side technique (Adjustment 1) and placing more emphasis on his winners (Adjustment 2).

It is, however, most difficult for an outsider to designate any specific adjustment for another individual. Cathy, Lupe, and Arnold could experiment with all the techniques and then concentrate on those that help the most.

# Case 24: Sensitivity

The authors suggest that Bernice stay where she is until she completes a formal course in supervision and/or managerial leadership. Once she has training, she will be in a better position to consider the demands of such a job in light of her own personality, values, and goals. It is quite possible that Bernice would agonize so deeply over making hard people decisions that she would be ineffective as a supervisor.

Not everyone who is highly effective at human relations should become a supervisor. Many people who were exceptionally competent at working with people at the nonmanagement level have failed completely in a leadership role. In this respect, it would appear that management may have made a mistake in inviting Bernice to become a supervisor at this early stage. They may be trading their best producer for a supervisor who won't be happy and may leave the organization. This would be a loss to all concerned. On the other hand, with time and experience, people change, mature, and need new challenges. A successful management career is not out of the question for Bernice and may become a very rewarding and fulfilling career choice for her.

# Index